THE GENIUS KID'S GUIDE TO THE OLYMPICS

BY CHRÖS MCDOUGALL

North Star
KIDS

TABLE OF CONTENTS

Every four years, athletes from around the world come together to compete against each other in different sports. The competitions are intense, but the mood is festive and peaceful. These competitions are known as the Olympic Games. The name and concept date back to ancient times.

Around 3,000 years ago, people from Greece met in the city of Olympia. They had gathered for a religious and sporting festival. Named for the host city, the event was called the Olympic Games. The first record of the ancient Games is from 776 BCE. Additional Olympics were held every four years until around 393 CE.

The Olympic rings are the most recognizable sign of the Games. They symbolize five continents coming together.

In the ancient Olympics, most participants were soldiers.

The ancient Olympic Games were an important event for the Greek people. At the time, Greece was made up of several city-states that reached as far as Italy, North Africa, and Asia Minor. Although they were all part of Greece, these states were not always unified. At times they were at war with one another. However, when it was time for the Olympics, a truce was called so all free Greek men could come together in Olympia.

At their heart, the ancient Olympics were a religious ceremony to honor the

THE PANHELLENIC GAMES

Following the creation of the ancient Olympics, three similar festivals were founded in other parts of Greece. These were called the Panhellenic Games. The Pythian Games were held in Delphi. The Isthmian Games were on the Isthmus of Corinth. The Nemean Games took place in Nemea. Each event celebrated one of the Greek gods.

Greek god Zeus. However, the sporting competitions were central to the gathering. Any free Greek man was allowed to compete. Women, enslaved people, and non-Greeks were banned from attending. The athletes competed naked. They took part in contests such as footraces, boxing, and equestrian events. Athletes also competed in the pentathlon, which was a competition consisting of discus, long jump, javelin, running, and wrestling. The winner of each Olympic competition received a crown made of olive tree branches.

The format and sports in the ancient Olympics changed over the years. The event peaked in popularity around 500 BCE. Eventually, the Roman Empire took control of Greece. During the next several centuries, the Games began to lose importance. Then they stopped completely for more than 1,000 years.

The ancient Panathenaic Stadium in Athens was used as a venue for the first modern Olympics in 1896.

THE MODERN OLYMPIC GAMES

Over the years, people tried to restart the Olympics. Some even got as far as holding events, but none of them stuck. In the late 1800s, a French-born educator named Pierre de Coubertin tried to breathe life into the Olympics. He envisioned a rekindled Olympic Games as a time when people from different countries could come together peacefully through sports. Achieving that dream was not easy, however.

At first, sports officials and the Greek government weren't interested in restarting the Games, but organizers kept trying. Led by Coubertin, the first modern Olympic Games were held in 1896 in Athens, Greece. It was a much smaller event than later Games. Athletes from 14 countries competed in 43 events. These included cycling, fencing, swimming, track and field, and wrestling. Many people who took part considered the Games to be a success. The next two Olympics nearly killed the new event, however. The 1900 Olympics were held in Paris, France. They were followed by the 1904 Games in St. Louis, Missouri. Both events were held alongside major exhibitions. That, along with poor planning, made the Olympics feel almost secondary.

James Connolly poses with an American flag at the 1896 Olympic Games in Athens. With a win in the triple jump, he became the first champion in the modern Olympics.

Following a 1906 competition in Athens that isn't considered part of the Olympic Games, the 1908 Olympics were held in London, England. It was here that the opening ceremony, including a parade of nations, first took place. The successful London Games helped to restore the Olympics. However, that momentum was soon tested when the 1916 Olympics were canceled due to World War I (1914–1918). The Games survived, though, and the first postwar Olympics took place in 1920 in Antwerp, Belgium. They were considered a success. Antwerp was also when symbols and traditions such as the Olympic flag, the Olympic oath, and the release of pigeons at the opening ceremony were introduced.

The Olympics continued expanding in other ways. Women had been barred from the 1896 Games. They participated for the first time in 1900. Women's sports have been growing at the Olympics ever since.

US athlete Eddie Eagan won gold in the light heavyweight boxing event at the 1920 Olympics. Twelve years later he also won a gold medal in bobsled.

In 1924, a separate Olympic Winter Games was created for sports contested on snow and ice. Today, the Summer and Winter Games are organized so that one event happens every two years. This allows each to have time in the spotlight.

CHALLENGES AND CONTROVERSIES

The goal of the Olympic movement is to bring people together through sports to create a better and more peaceful world. Politics, war, and other controversies have sometimes interfered with that mission. For example, in 1936, the German government used the Summer Olympics for propaganda and to help hide the horrible acts it was committing—acts that eventually led to World War II (1939–1945). The International Olympic Committee (IOC) had to cancel the Games scheduled during the war.

At other times, countries were prevented from competing in the Olympics for political reasons. Countries have also boycotted the Games to protest the host country. This was most notable in 1980. The United States and 64 other countries refused to participate in the Summer Games in Moscow, Russia. They were upset that the Soviet Union, which Russia was part of, had invaded Afghanistan. In response, the Soviet Union led a boycott of the 1984 Summer Games in Los Angeles, California.

The Olympic Games have also experienced violence. In 1972,

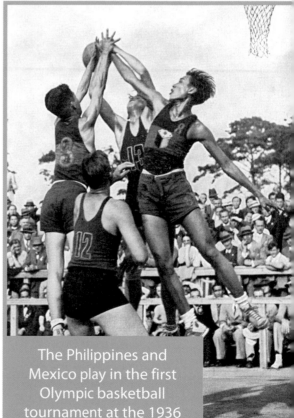

The Philippines and Mexico play in the first Olympic basketball tournament at the 1936 Games in Berlin, Germany.

Palestinian terrorists snuck into the Olympic Village in Munich, West Germany. They killed 11 members of the Israeli team. In 1996, a man detonated a bomb in the Olympic Park in Atlanta, Georgia. Two people were killed and more than 100 were hurt.

Doping has also become a constant challenge in sports. Some athletes illegally use substances to improve their performances. Before competing in the Olympics, athletes have to

Doping is seen as an unfair way for an athlete to get an advantage over the competition.

take drug tests. People are disqualified from the Olympics if performance-enhancing drugs are found in their systems.

Through the years, the IOC has struggled to control rising costs. Hosting the Games is very expensive. The host city must often construct new buildings and renovate others. Some cities add public transportation so people can easily get to events. They also must pay for security and other operations. Tokyo, Japan, hosted the 2020 Olympics. The city expected to spend around $7.4 billion. The Games ended up costing $15.4 billion.

Due to the COVID-19 pandemic, the 2020 Tokyo Games were the first Olympics to be postponed. COVID-19 is a disease spread by a virus. More than four million people around the world had died from it by the time the rescheduled Games took place in 2021. Many people questioned whether the Games should be held at all, since Japan was struggling to contain the virus. Although the rescheduled Games took place a year late, the event was still marketed as the 2020 Olympics.

The virus that causes COVID-19 can spread easily through the air. Athletes wore masks when not actively competing in the 2020 Olympics.

GROWING AND CHANGING

The Olympics always find a way to keep going. The event continues to change and adapt to the times. This can be seen in attitudes toward women's sports. While women were first allowed to compete in 1900, their participation was very limited in the early years. Many people at the time believed women could not handle difficult physical activity. Those ideas have long since been proven wrong. Today, the IOC tries to create equal opportunities for men and women at the Games.

Until the 1970s, the Olympics were limited to amateur athletes. Athletes who were paid for competing in sports weren't eligible. That rule created financial hardships for

Olympians. This practice slowly changed in the 1980s. Today, most Olympic athletes are professionals. This change allows athletes to earn more money. In some cases, this lets them compete longer or extend their fame outside of the Olympics.

Additional revenue has helped the Olympics grow as an event too. Early Olympic Games usually lost money. A new model introduced for the 1984 Summer Games put the Olympics on stable financial footing. Today, TV broadcasters pay billions of dollars for the rights to show the Games. Major companies pay money to sponsor the Olympics, allowing them to use the Olympic rings on their products. All the while, the Olympic sports program continues to change with the times as well.

Despite some controversies surrounding the Olympics, fans keep coming back to watch athletes such as gymnast Simone Biles.

All of these developments have helped ensure the Olympics remain a cherished event. Every couple of years, the Games bring the world together for a celebration of peace, unity, and sports.

SUMMER SPORTS

The Summer Games are officially called the Olympic Games. They are the original version of the Olympics founded in 1896. The Summer Games have more sports than the Winter Games.

While traditional sports such as fencing, swimming, and wrestling have been around as long as the modern Olympics, new summer sports such as beach volleyball (1996), BMX cycling (2008), and 3x3 basketball (2020) have helped the Games stay current and reach new audiences.

LOS ANGELES, CALIFORNIA (1932, 1984, 2028)

ST. LOUIS, MISSOURI (1904)

MONTREAL, CANADA (1976)

ATLANTA, GEORGIA (1996)

MEXICO CITY, MEXICO (1968)

RIO DE JANEIRO, BRAZIL (2016)

SUMMER GAMES HOST CITIES

Many of the world's biggest cities have hosted the modern Summer Games. The only populated continent that hasn't hosted the Summer Games is Africa.

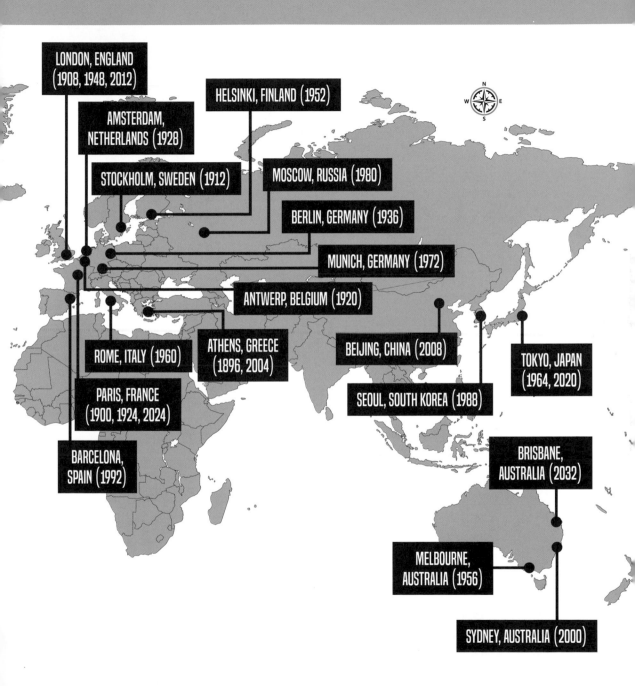

LONDON, ENGLAND (1908, 1948, 2012)

HELSINKI, FINLAND (1952)

AMSTERDAM, NETHERLANDS (1928)

STOCKHOLM, SWEDEN (1912)

MOSCOW, RUSSIA (1980)

BERLIN, GERMANY (1936)

MUNICH, GERMANY (1972)

ANTWERP, BELGIUM (1920)

ROME, ITALY (1960)

ATHENS, GREECE (1896, 2004)

BEIJING, CHINA (2008)

TOKYO, JAPAN (1964, 2020)

PARIS, FRANCE (1900, 1924, 2024)

SEOUL, SOUTH KOREA (1988)

BARCELONA, SPAIN (1992)

BRISBANE, AUSTRALIA (2032)

MELBOURNE, AUSTRALIA (1956)

SYDNEY, AUSTRALIA (2000)

ARCHERY

In the Olympics, archers begin with a 72-arrow ranking round. Then they compete in a single-elimination bracket to determine who wins the bronze, silver, and gold medals.

ABOUT THE COMPETITION

Olympic archers use recurve bows to shoot at targets 70 meters (230 feet) away. Arrows get points based on how close they are to the centers of the targets. In the Olympics, there are both individual and team archery competitions for men and women. There's also a mixed team competition.

ORIGIN

Dating back to ancient times, archery was used in warfare and for hunting. It was also used in competitions. This makes it one of the oldest sports. The first competitions were held in Egypt during the 1500s BCE, and more followed in China.

THROUGHOUT THE YEARS

Archery appeared in the Olympics in 1900. This event was held three more times through 1920. In 1972, the sport returned to the Olympics with a men's and women's event. Team events followed in 1988, and mixed teams were added in 2020.

Kim Soo-Nyung eyes her target during the 2020 Games.

ICONS

South Korean women have dominated the Olympic archery competition since 1972. They've won nine of the 13 individual gold medals through 2020. No female archer has won more medals than Kim Soo-Nyung. She won six medals, four of them gold, between 1988 and 2000. Hubert Van Innis of Belgium is the most decorated male archer. He won six gold medals and ten total medals in just two Games, which took place in 1900 and 1920.

China's Lin Dan participates in the bronze-medal match in the 2016 Games.

ABOUT THE COMPETITION

In badminton, athletes on opposite sides of a net use rackets to hit an object, called a shuttlecock. Players earn points when the shuttlecock lands inside the opponent's court. One side can also earn a point if the opponent hits the shuttlecock into the net or out of bounds. Olympic badminton has singles, doubles, and mixed doubles competitions.

ORIGIN

Badminton was originally known as Poona. The sport was invented in India. It grew in popularity in the late 1800s after English soldiers brought it home. In 1873, they demonstrated the sport at an estate called Badminton House. Before long, it began spreading around the world.

THROUGHOUT THE YEARS

Badminton became an Olympic sport at the 1992 Games in Barcelona, Spain. Athletes from China, Indonesia, and South Korea have won most of the sport's medals.

ICONS

This fast-paced sport has produced many stars. Few can compare to Lin Dan of China. The lefty is known as "Super Dan." He won a men's singles gold medal on home soil in 2008. Then he defended that title in 2012. China's Zhang Ning became the first woman to win back-to-back singles gold medals. She did so in 2004 and 2008.

Brian Yang of Canada reaches for the shuttlecock during the 2020 Olympics.

19

BASKETBALL

ABOUT THE COMPETITION

In basketball, teams of five players try to score points by shooting a ball through a hoop. Each basket made is worth two points—unless it's shot from outside the three-point line, in which case it's worth three points. In the Olympics, basketball games are 40 minutes long. They are divided into four equal quarters.

ORIGIN

In 1891, Canadian James Naismith was working as a physical education instructor at a YMCA in Massachusetts. He needed an indoor activity for his students during the cold winter months. Naismith decided to hang two peach baskets on opposite sides of the gym. The students then tried to toss balls into the baskets. With that, basketball was born.

3X3 BASKETBALL

Basketball is one of the most accessible team sports. People play for fun in parks and gyms around the world. You don't always need a full-size team to play, either. Starting at the 2020 Games, men and women had separate 3x3 basketball competitions. In 3x3, teams play a half-court game to 21 points or for ten minutes, whichever comes first. Baskets count for one or two points. In the 2020 Olympics, the United States won gold in the women's competition while Latvia won on the men's side.

Team USA's Angel McCoughtry sails to the basket to score against Australia in the 2012 Olympic semifinals. Team USA went on to win gold.

THROUGHOUT THE YEARS

By the early 1900s, basketball was spreading around the United States. It was included as a demonstration sport at the 1904 Olympics. In 1936, it was welcomed as a full medal sport. A women's event debuted 40 years later, in 1976.

ICONS

No matter the era, the United States has dominated Olympic basketball. One of the greatest US men's teams competed in the 1960 Olympics. It was led by four future basketball Hall of Famers, including Jerry Lucas and Oscar Robertson. The Americans beat their eight opponents by an average of 42.4 points. However, no team compares to the 1992 "Dream Team." That year, National Basketball Association (NBA) athletes were able to play in the Olympics for the first time. All of the biggest stars showed up. This time, 11 future Hall of Famers played, including Magic Johnson and Michael Jordan. The Dream Team not only dominated the competition but also brought newfound global attention to the game.

As good as the US men were in the years that followed, the US women

were even better. Starting on home soil in 1996 in Atlanta, the Americans began a streak of seven consecutive gold medals. Center Lisa Leslie starred on four of those teams, winning her fourth gold medal in 2008. Teammates Sue Bird and Diana Taurasi took over from there. At the 2020 Games, each won their fifth gold medal to become the most decorated Olympic basketball players.

NBA star LeBron James won three Olympic medals with Team USA, including gold in 2008 and 2012.

BOXING

Great Britain's Frazer Clarke, *right*, lands a punch on France's Mourad Aliev during a super heavyweight boxing match in the 2020 Games.

ABOUT THE COMPETITION

Boxing is a straightforward combat sport. Two opponents wearing padded gloves use their fists to try to land blows on each other. Judges score how successful they are over three rounds. Matches can end early if one boxer cannot continue. Boxers are matched together in weight classes. This helps make sure no opponent has a major physical advantage.

ORIGIN

Boxing crowned its first Olympic champion in 688 BCE at the ancient Games in Greece. Later, Roman soldiers were known to box as well. Modern boxing came out of England in the late 1600s. The sport grew in popularity in the late 1800s after new rules were adopted, including one requiring gloves.

THROUGHOUT THE YEARS

Boxing has been an Olympic sport since 1904, although it was not held in 1912. A women's competition was added at the 2012 Olympics. Until 2016, only amateurs were allowed to compete in boxing.

ICONS

In 1960, an 18-year-old American named Cassius Clay won the light heavyweight gold medal. He went on to become the professional superstar known as Muhammad Ali. Another talented American, Claressa Shields, competed in the middleweight class. With quickness and punishing punches, she won gold medals in 2008 and 2012.

US boxer Claressa Shields shows off her two Olympic gold medals.

CANOE

Peter Kauzer of Slovenia navigates the white-water course at the 2016 Olympics.

ABOUT THE COMPETITION

Canoe athletes use paddles to navigate canoes or kayaks in races. The Olympics feature canoe slalom and canoe sprint events. Slalom takes place on a white-water course. Paddlers guide their boats through gates while competing one at a time. The slalom course is roughly 250 meters (820 feet) long. In sprint, the athletes race together across flat water. Sprint races range from 200 to 1,000 meters (656 to 3,281 feet).

ORIGIN

People have traveled by water in canoes for thousands of years. The first flat-water canoe races took place in the mid-1800s in the United Kingdom. Slalom racing originated in the 1930s in Switzerland.

THROUGHOUT THE YEARS

After debuting as an Olympic demonstration sport in 1924, flat-water canoe became a full Olympic sport in 1936. Women's events were added 12 years later. The events have changed over the years. Slalom was first held at the 1972 Olympics. It became a permanent Olympic feature in 1992.

ICONS

Birgit Fischer-Schmidt raced in her sixth Olympics in 2004. The German paddler has 12 Olympic medals—eight of which are gold. This is the most of any sprint canoeist. In canoe slalom, Slovakian twin brothers Peter and Pavol Hochschorner competed together. They won three gold medals plus a bronze between 2000 and 2012.

Australia's Alyssa Bull and Alyce Wood compete in the double kayak at the 2020 Olympics.

ABOUT THE COMPETITION

The Olympics feature four kinds of cycling races. They are BMX, mountain, road, and track. BMX cyclists also compete in a freestyle event.

The goal of any cycling race is to cross the finish line first. How the rider gets there differs in each event. BMX riders have compact bikes. They ride them over a short course filled with jumps, hills, and banked turns. Mountain bikes are big and durable. Riders must be able to go over rocks and other obstacles. Olympic mountain bike races are long, often taking more than an hour and a half.

The Games have two road cycling races for men and women. Riders compete one at a time in the time trial. In the road race, riders start together and travel a long distance. Just as the name suggests, these races take place on everyday roads.

Mountain bikers must navigate difficult off-road courses.

Track cyclists can reach speeds of 40 miles per hour (64 kmh).

The fastest races happen on the track. It is a banked 250-meter (820 foot) oval. There are events for single riders and teams. Some focus on sprints and others on endurance.

The newest Olympic cycling event is BMX freestyle. In this sport, riders are judged for the tricks they do using the elements inside a park. These elements include walls, box jumps, and spines.

ORIGIN

Bicycles have been used for transportation since the early to mid-1800s. The first bike race took place in 1868 near Paris. It wasn't long before road and track races were being held around the world. Eventually people began taking their bikes off-road. In the 1970s, the first mountain bikers rode through the wilderness in California. It was around this time, and also in California, that BMX bikes became popular.

THROUGHOUT THE YEARS

Cycling is one of five sports that has been part of every Summer Olympics. Road and track cycling have been there from the start in 1896, with a few exceptions. Mountain biking made its Olympic debut in 1996. BMX racing was added in 2008, followed by freestyle in 2020.

ICONS

British riders Chris Hoy and Jason Kenny lead all track cyclists with six gold medals. Each won two on home soil at the 2012 Olympics. Team USA's Kristin Armstrong won her record-tying third road cycling gold medal in 2016. Maris Strombergs of Latvia won the first men's BMX racing gold medal in 2008. Then he defended it in 2012. In mountain biking, Swiss rider Nino Schurter earned a bronze medal in 2008. Then he got a silver in 2012. In 2016, he finally won gold.

Great Britain's Charlotte Worthington won gold in the BMX freestyle event at the 2020 Olympics.

DIVING

ABOUT THE COMPETITION

In diving, athletes perform acrobatic skills while plunging headfirst into the water. They are judged based on the dive's beauty, difficulty, and entry. In the Olympics, the diving events are held from either a 3-meter (9.8 foot) springboard or a 10-meter (33 foot) platform. The springboard allows divers to jump higher into the air before falling to the pool. A platform does not provide any bounce.

For men and women, there are individual and synchronized events on each board. In synchronized diving, teams of two divers are also judged based on how similar their movements are.

Divers strive to make the smallest splash possible when entering the water.

In the Olympics, female divers accumulate points over five dives. Male divers have six dives.

ORIGIN

Diving originated in the 1800s as an alternate activity for gymnasts. It first became popular in Germany and Sweden. Diving had spread to the United Kingdom and beyond by the 1900s.

Synchronized divers practice their moves together.

THROUGHOUT THE YEARS

Known at the time as "fancy diving," a men's springboard event was included in the 1904 Olympics. A men's platform event was added four years later. The first women's event debuted four years after that. Early Olympic diving used different formats and equipment. The familiar 3- and 10-meter events have been part of the Olympics since 1928. Synchronized diving has been part of the Olympics since 2000.

ICONS

Although similar, the 3-meter and 10-meter events require different skills. Elite divers typically excel at one or the other. Southern California native Pat McCormick set a new standard when she won both events in consecutive Olympics, in 1952 and 1956. That feat was called the double-double.

Only one person has matched McCormick's double-double. Greg Louganis would have been a favorite to win a gold medal in 1980 had the United States not boycotted those Olympics. He made up for lost time when he swept the men's events in 1984 and 1988. His 1988 springboard win came after he shockingly hit his head on the board during the preliminary round.

After years of US dominance in diving, China emerged as the powerhouse during the 1990s. Wu Minxia is the sport's most decorated athlete. She won seven medals, including five gold, from 2004 to 2016. Three other Chinese divers—Chen Ruolin, Guo Jingjing, and Fu Mingxia—each won at least four gold medals and at least five overall.

Greg Louganis competes in the springboard diving event at the 1988 Summer Games. He won the gold medal, becoming the first man to sweep the springboard and platform competitions at back-to-back Olympics.

ABOUT THE COMPETITION

In equestrian events, riders on horseback compete in dressage, jumping, and eventing. It is the only Olympic sport to include animals as participants.

French for *training*, dressage involves the horse performing intricate maneuvers. In jumping, the rider and horse must navigate a course while clearing a series of obstacles such as walls and water features. Eventing tests the all-around ability of both rider and horse through jumping, dressage, and cross-country competitions. There are both individual and team competitions in all three events.

ORIGIN

The Greeks used horses in battles during ancient times. Horses also appeared in the ancient Olympics as part of chariot races. All three modern equestrian events originated from military training.

Germany's Kristina Sprehe won the first of her three dressage medals in 2012.

China's Alex Hua Tian competes in the jumping competition in the 2016 Games.

THROUGHOUT THE YEARS

Equestrian events were first held in the 1900 Olympics in Paris. After being left out of the next two Summer Games, the sport has been in the Olympic program continuously since 1912. Only male military officers were allowed to compete through 1948.

ICONS

German riders have shined brightest in Olympic equestrian. In 2016, Isabell Werth became the most decorated athlete in the sport. Following the 2020 Olympics she had 12 medals, seven of which were gold.

A ROYAL FAMILY

Princess Anne of England was a talented equestrian. She competed in eventing at the 1976 Olympics in Montreal. Her daughter, Zara Phillips, won an Olympic silver medal in team eventing at the 2012 Games in London.

FENCING

Fencers need to use precise movements to strike their opponents.

ABOUT THE COMPETITION

In fencing, two athletes with swords attempt to strike each other. An athlete earns points for striking his or her opponent in certain target areas. Whoever earns more points wins.

Fencing includes three types of swords. Each discipline has slightly different rules. In foil fencing, an athlete scores points by pressing the tip of the blade into the opponent's torso. The person is not allowed to strike other areas, such as the arms, legs, or head.

An épée fencer may strike any part of the opponent's body. However, the épée sword is much heavier than a foil. This makes it more difficult to control.

Saber is the most aggressive fencing style. An athlete scores points using both the tip and sides of the blade. Anywhere above the waist, except the hands, is fair game.

Special equipment helps make sure the athletes don't get hurt. Electric sensors within the equipment determine if a fencer's sword made contact within the target area. The Olympics has both individual and team events for all three weapons.

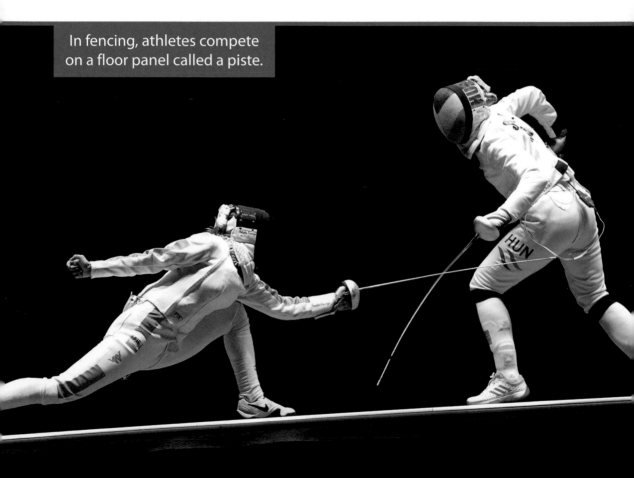

In fencing, athletes compete on a floor panel called a piste.

ORIGIN

People have fought with swords for thousands of years. The earliest known depiction of fencing was from around 1190 BCE in Egypt. The modern version of fencing originated more than 2,000 years later in Europe. Germans and Italians claim to have fenced as part of military training as early as the 1300s. By the late 1800s, fencing was becoming popular as a sport, with the foil being the weapon of choice.

THROUGHOUT THE YEARS

Fencing is one of five sports to have been part of every modern Olympics. The first Olympic fencing competitions were only for men. Women's foil was added in 1924, followed by épée in 1996 and saber in 2004.

ICONS

Nedo Nadi won the individual foil gold medal in 1912. In 1920, he returned to the Olympics with a performance for the ages. In addition to defending his title in individual foil and adding another gold medal in individual saber, Nadi led the Italians to team gold medals in épée, foil, and saber. He remains the only fencer to have medaled in all three weapons.

Many great fencers followed Nadi. Hungary's Aladar Gerevich won ten Olympic medals, including six golds in a row in men's team saber from 1932 to 1960. That is the longest gold medal streak in any Olympic event.

Valentina Vezzali stands out among many great Italian women's fencers. She won six gold medals between 1996 and 2012. This included three in individual foil.

Lee Kiefer celebrates after winning gold in foil during the 2020 Games.

FIELD HOCKEY

ABOUT THE COMPETITION

Similar to its counterpart on ice, field hockey involves teams of players using sticks to try to send balls into the opponent's goal. Games are played over four 15-minute quarters on a turf field. Each team has 11 players on the field at a time, including one goalie.

With its fourth gold medal in 2020, the Netherlands, *shown in orange*, passed Australia for the most Olympic titles in women's field hockey.

ORIGIN

In many parts of the world, field hockey is simply called hockey. That's because field hockey is actually much older than ice hockey. In fact, people were playing a version of field hockey as far back as 4,000 years ago in Egypt. The modern game developed in the mid-1800s in England.

THROUGHOUT THE YEARS

A men's field hockey tournament was held at the 1908 Olympics. It has remained on the Olympic program except in 1924. Women's field hockey made its Olympic debut in 1980.

India's men's team brought home a bronze medal at the 2020 Olympics.

ICONS

India is the world's second most populated country. However, it typically doesn't have a large presence in the Olympics. One exception is in field hockey. At the 2020 Olympics, India won its 12th medal in men's field hockey. Among them were eight golds. On the women's side, the Netherlands won its ninth medal in the 2020 Games.

ABOUT THE COMPETITION

A golfer uses clubs to hit a ball from a starting point into a hole. The goal is to strike the ball as few times as possible. A round of golf features 18 holes. The Olympic competition has four rounds. Using stroke-play scoring, the golfer with the fewest total shots over the four rounds wins.

ORIGIN

No one is certain when people began playing golf. Similar games existed in Europe as early as the 1200s. However, most people credit Scotland with developing the modern game beginning in the 1400s.

Klara Spilkova of the Czech Republic lines up her shot during the 2016 Games.

THROUGHOUT THE YEARS

Men's golf was included in the second and third modern Olympics, in 1900 and 1904. After that the sport was removed from the program until 2016. It returned with events for men and women.

ICONS

Inbee Park had already established herself as one of the world's top golfers. At the 2016 Olympic debut of women's golf, she proved it again on the biggest stage. The South Korean star played consistent golf over all four rounds. She finished 16-under par and won the gold medal. In men's golf that year, Justin Rose of the Great Britain and Northern Ireland Olympic Team— commonly called Team Great Britain— won the gold medal.

Team USA's Xander Schauffele won the men's gold medal at the 2020 Olympics.

GYMNASTICS

ABOUT THE COMPETITION

There are three gymnastics disciplines in the Olympics: artistic, rhythmic, and trampoline. When most people talk about Olympic gymnastics, they are referring to artistic. This competition is when a gymnast performs a routine on an apparatus. Judges score the gymnast based on difficulty and execution.

Women's gymnastics features events on the balance beam, floor, uneven bars, and vault. Men's gymnastics also has floor exercise and vault, plus

RHYTHMIC GYMNASTICS

Rhythmic gymnastics focuses on artistry and style more than technical ability and athleticism. During a competition, a gymnast performs routines to music while handling a hoop, ball, pair of clubs, or ribbon. There is an individual all-around and group competition in the Olympics, with both being women-only events.

Rhythmic gymnastics has been an Olympic sport since 1984. During that time, Russia has dominated. Following the 2020 Olympics, Russia—including the Soviet Union and the Unified Team—had won 12 rhythmic gymnastics gold medals.

Suni Lee's performance on the uneven bars helped her win the women's all-around gold medal at the 2020 Games. She was the first Hmong American to compete in the Olympics.

horizontal bar, parallel bars, pommel horse, and still rings. In the Olympics, gymnasts compete for gold medals in each event. In addition, there are all-around and team competitions for both men and women.

Each apparatus tests a gymnast in different ways. The top all-around gymnast must possess great ability in areas such as balance, strength, power, coordination, tumbling, and stamina.

ORIGIN

Some of the ideas for gymnastics originated in ancient times. However, the forms practiced in the ancient Olympics and elsewhere don't much resemble the sport people know today. Modern gymnastics began to emerge during the early 1800s in Germany. Athletic clubs and schools held individual exhibitions. The sport continued to grow and develop into the early 1900s.

Tim Daggett of the United States performs a skill on the rings at the 1984 Olympic Games.

TRAMPOLINE

Trampoline gymnastics was added to the Olympics in 2000. In this sport, athletes on trampolines launch themselves high into the air and perform daring twists, spins, and somersaults. There are individual events for men and women. Canada's Rosie MacLennan won back-to-back gold medals in 2012 and 2016. China's Dong Dong has won four medals, making him the most decorated athlete in the sport.

THROUGHOUT THE YEARS

Artistic gymnastics has been in every Olympics since the first one in 1896. However, the sport looked different in its early days. Among the early events were rope climbing, club swinging, and side horse. The modern Olympic men's program dates back to 1924. The first Olympic women's gymnastics events were held in 1928.

One of the biggest adjustments in recent years was the change in scoring. Instead of scoring routines up to ten, the sport implemented a new open-ended system in 2006. The new system was intended to better recognize difficulty.

Romania's Nadia Comăneci dismounts from the uneven bars after her perfect routine at the 1976 Olympic Games.

Team USA's Gabby Douglas soars above the balance beam during the 2012 London Olympics. She went on to win gold in the women's all-around.

ICONS

Several women have defined the sport across different eras. During the 1950s and 1960s, the Soviet Union's Larisa Latynina won 18 medals, nine of which were gold. No woman, and only one man, has won more Olympic medals across all sports.

In 1972, Soviet gymnast Olga Korbut helped bring the sport into the mainstream with her daring routines and natural charisma. Four years later, Nadia Comăneci took the sport to even greater heights with her performance in Montreal. The Romanian teenager performed such an exquisite bars routine that the judges awarded her a perfect ten. That had never happened before in the Olympics, so the scoreboard wasn't even set up to display it correctly. Combining innovative skills and stellar form, Comăneci ended up scoring seven perfect tens on her way to winning three gold medals. Four years later she won two more. In total, Comăneci won nine Olympic medals.

The United States has emerged as the dominant country in women's gymnastics. That began in 1984, when Mary Lou Retton won the all-around gold medal. In 1996, a squad nicknamed "the Magnificent Seven" won the team gold medal. The US women have won team medals at every Olympics since, including gold in 2012 and 2016.

From 2004 through 2020, US women also won five consecutive all-around titles. They were Carly Patterson, Nastia Liukin, Gabby Douglas,

Simone Biles, and Suni Lee.

Combining power with unrivaled technical ability, Biles won four gold medals and a bronze medal in 2016. She was favored to win several more gold medals at the 2020 Games. However, she developed a condition in which she became unable to control her body in the air. As a result, Biles had to withdraw from all but two events. She still left Tokyo with a silver medal in the team event and a bronze medal on the balance beam.

Simone Biles, *left*, and US teammate Aly Raisman celebrate after Biles won gold and Raisman won silver in the 2016 Olympic all-around final.

Many people admired Biles for opening up about her struggles with mental health during the Games.

Japan's Sawao Kato is the most decorated male gymnast. He won his eighth gold medal, and twelfth overall, in 1976. One of the most dominant Olympic men's gymnastics performances came in 1992. That year, Vitaly Scherbo won a record six gold medals. Competing for the Unified Team—a team of athletes from the former Soviet

republics—the only events he didn't win were floor exercise
and horizontal bar. Four years later, while competing for Belarus,
Scherbo won four more bronze medals.

Kohei Uchimura of Japan set a new standard a decade later.
After winning all-around silver in 2008, he won gold at the next two
Olympics. In four Olympics he won seven total medals.

HANDBALL

Fans are often drawn to the fast pace and exciting action of team handball.

ABOUT THE COMPETITION

Played on an indoor court with goals on each end, handball combines elements of basketball, soccer, and water polo to create a fast-paced team sport. Players move the ball by dribbling or passing. They score by throwing the ball into the opposing net. In a 60-minute handball game, it's not uncommon to see as many as 60 goals.

ORIGIN

The first handball games were played in the late 1800s in northern Europe. The sport gained popularity there into the early 1900s. However, the game was originally played outdoors with 11 players on each team.

THROUGHOUT THE YEARS

Field handball became an Olympic sport in 1936. It wasn't until the 1972 Olympics that the sport moved to an indoor court and the current seven-a-side format debuted. Four years later, the first Olympic women's handball tournament was held.

ICONS

Between the former Soviet Union, the 1992 Unified Team, and the Russian teams that followed, that country has produced 13 Olympic handball medals—seven of them gold. Andrey Lavrov was part of the men's gold-medal teams in 1988, 1992, and 2000. Oh Seong-Ok of South Korea became the first woman to claim four Olympic handball medals. She helped lead her team to gold in 1992.

Handball can be an aggressive sport.

ABOUT THE COMPETITION

Judo is a traditional Japanese combat sport. It features one-on-one bouts where athletes known as judokas use grappling and throwing techniques to overcome their opponents. Although the word *judo* means "gentle way" in Japanese, the sport can be aggressive.

ORIGIN

Judo can be traced back to Dr. Kanō Jigorō. He founded judo in 1882 by taking parts of other ancient Japanese martial arts and combining them. Originally designed to be a safe activity, judo grew to become more competitive over time.

The United States' Ronda Rousey, *right*, battles Germany's Annett Boehm during the 2008 Olympic judo competition.

THROUGHOUT THE YEARS

Fittingly, judo made its Olympic debut in 1964, when the Games were held in Tokyo. Men's judo has been a continuous Olympic sport since 1972. Women have been part of Olympic judo since 1992.

ICONS

Perhaps unsurprisingly, Japan has won more Olympic judo medals than any other country. Ryoko Tani made a mistake at her first Olympics in 1992 and ended up with a silver medal. As the heavy favorite in 1996, she again finished in second place. Finally, in 2000, she won gold. Then she added another gold medal and a bronze medal in 2004 and 2008. Only two men, Japan's Tadahiro Nomura and France's Teddy Riner, have won three Olympic gold medals in judo.

Isao Inokuma, *right*, was one of three Japanese judokas to win gold medals at the 1964 Olympics.

MODERN PENTATHLON

The modern pentathlon tests an athlete's all-around sporting ability.

ABOUT THE COMPETITION

The modern pentathlon consists of five sports. Athletes first earn points in competitions for fencing, swimming, and equestrian show jumping. Then they take part in a combined cross-country run and target shooting event. The runners start in order of most to fewest points earned over the first three events. At four checkpoints they must hit all five shooting targets, or wait 50 seconds, before continuing the run. Whoever crosses the finish line first wins.

ORIGIN

Pentathlon was included in the ancient Olympics to determine the most complete athlete. The original five sports were running, jumping, spear throwing, discus, and wrestling.

THROUGHOUT THE YEARS

The modern pentathlon debuted at the 1912 Olympics with the five sports included today. However, the event format has changed many times over the years. In 1996, it was shortened from four days to one. A women's event was added in 2000. More recently, prior to the 2012 Games, running and shooting were made into a combined event.

ICONS

Only two men have won two individual gold medals in modern pentathlon. They are Lars Hall of Sweden (1952, 1956) and Andrey Moiseyev of Russia (2004, 2008). Hall was also the first winner without a military background. Great Britain's Steph Cook used a blazing run to become the first women's winner in 2000.

The modern pentathlon format has changed over the years.

ROWING

Greece's Stefanos Ntouskos won gold in the men's single sculls in the 2020 Games.

ABOUT THE COMPETITION

In rowing, athletes use oars to propel boats across a straight, 2,000-meter (6,562 foot) flat water course. The Olympic program features races for one-, two-, four-, and eight-person boats. The eight also includes a coxswain. Rowers sit backward in the boat. In sculling events, rowers hold an oar in each hand. In sweep events, each rower holds just one oar using both hands. Some events, called lightweight events, have maximum weight restrictions for the crew.

ORIGIN

Rowboats were used for transportation in ancient Egypt, Greece, and Rome. Rowing as a sport likely began in the late 1600s in England. By the mid-1800s, it was growing in popularity across Europe and North America.

THROUGHOUT THE YEARS

Rowing was supposed to be part of the first modern Olympics in 1896, but a bad storm forced the event to be canceled. It was back on the schedule in 1900, though, and never left. Women's events were added in 1976.

The Canadian women's eight boat team won gold in the 2020 Olympics.

ICONS

Only three athletes have won five Olympic gold medals in rowing: Great Britain's Sir Steve Redgrave (1984–2000) and Romania's Elisabeta Lipa (1984–2004) and Georgeta Damian-Andrunache (2000–2008). Lipa's eight total rowing medals is a record. The US women's eight boat was unbeaten at global championships from 2006 to 2016, a streak that included three Olympic gold medals.

RUGBY SEVENS

ABOUT THE COMPETITION

Rugby sevens is a smaller version of traditional rugby. With seven players per side, rather than the full 15, sevens is a faster-paced game with lots of scoring. The objective is to score points by carrying the ball across the goal line for a try (five points) or by kicking it through goal posts (two or three points). An entire game is completed in just 14 minutes.

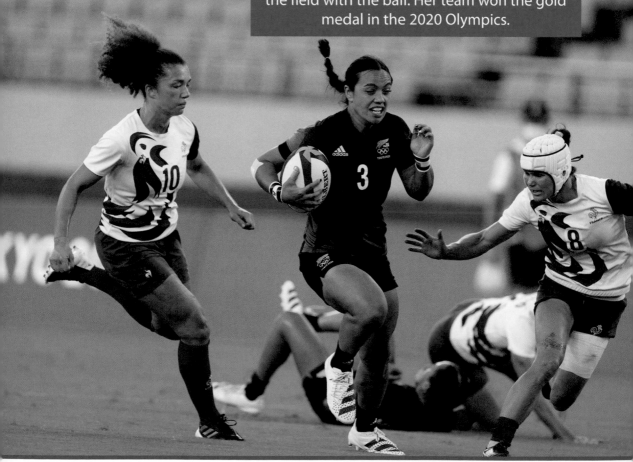

Stacey Fluhler of New Zealand races down the field with the ball. Her team won the gold medal in the 2020 Olympics.

ORIGIN

According to legend, rugby was founded in 1823 at Rugby School in the United Kingdom. By the 1900s, the sport had spread around the world. Rugby sevens is almost as old, having first been played in 1883 in Scotland. However, the seven-a-side game really took off in the early 2000s.

THROUGHOUT THE YEARS

Men's 15-a-side rugby was held at four Olympics

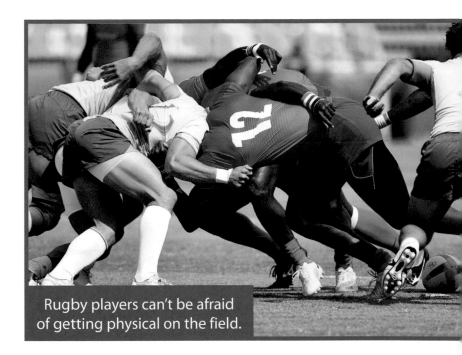

Rugby players can't be afraid of getting physical on the field.

between 1900 and 1924. That sport has thrived in several countries. The faster seven-a-side version helped expand the sport. By 2016, that growth included Olympic tournaments for men and women.

ICONS

In 2016, the tiny island nation of Fiji beat Great Britain in the men's final to win the country's first gold medal in any sport. Fiji won again in the 2020 Games. On the women's side, New Zealand won gold in the 2020 Olympics after claiming silver in 2016.

ABOUT THE COMPETITION

In sailing competitions, athletes race across ocean waters in boats propelled by the wind. The courses are shaped like a triangle to ensure sailors navigate wind from three directions. Different races are held for each class of boats. In the Olympics, sailors compete in a series of fleet races. Points are awarded from low to high based on finishing position. Points are doubled for the final race, called the medal race. Whoever has the fewest points at the end wins.

ORIGIN

People have been using sailboats for transportation since ancient times. Sail-powered boats, sometimes called yachts, were first used for leisure and racing in the 1600s in the Netherlands.

Americans Anna Weis and Riley Gibbs compete in the mixed Nacra 17 race during the 2020 Olympics.

Strong teamwork is essential for multiperson sailboats.

THROUGHOUT THE YEARS

Sailing has been part of every Olympics but one since 1900. The Olympic boat classes regularly change, but the one-man Finn boat has been contested since 1952. Though women had sailed in the Olympics from the start, the first event just for women was held in 1988.

ICONS

In 2012, Great Britain's Ben Ainslie won his fourth gold medal. That matched Denmark's Paul Elvstrom. Ainslie also became the first sailor to win a medal at five consecutive Olympics. His medals came in three different classes. Alessandra Sensini of Italy won her fourth windsurfing medal in 2008.

FIRST OLYMPIC FEMALE SAILOR

Swiss sailor Hélène de Pourtalès was the first woman to participate in the Olympics. She was also the first woman to earn an Olympic medal. She was part of sailing crews that won a gold and a silver medal in 1900.

ABOUT THE COMPETITION

Shooting tests athletes' abilities to hit targets with firearms. There are three shooting disciplines in the Olympics. In pistol and rifle events, shooters aim for still targets within a shooting range. Shotgun shooters must hit clay targets that fly through the air.

Yang Qian of China won gold in the 10-meter air rifle event in the 2020 Games.

ORIGIN

The first known use of a firearm was in the 1300s. People began using firearms for sport more than 500 years ago in Germany.

THROUGHOUT THE YEARS

Shooting appeared in the first modern Olympics in 1896. It has been in almost every Olympics since, although the shooting program has changed greatly over the years. Women were first allowed to compete in 1968. The first events specifically for women were held in 1984.

ICONS

American Kim Rhode was 17 years old when she won the double trap gold medal in 1996. She added a bronze and another gold medal at the next two Olympics. Then, when double trap was taken off the program, Rhode won three more medals—including another gold—at the next three Olympics in skeet shooting. Rhode became one of just two athletes to win medals at six Olympics in an individual sport. Fellow American Carl Osburn, with 11 medals from 1912 to 1924, is the sport's most decorated Olympian.

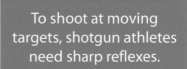

To shoot at moving targets, shotgun athletes need sharp reflexes.

Mia Hamm, *right*, led the US women to a gold medal in 1996 and again in 2004.

ABOUT THE COMPETITION

Soccer is the world's most popular sport. It involves two teams with 11 players each. Athletes try to score goals by sending the ball into the opponent's net. Except for the goalie, players cannot touch the ball with their hands or arms. Soccer is held on a large field. Games are 90 minutes long.

ORIGIN

Although similar foot-and-ball games existed in China as far back as 2,000 years ago, modern soccer dates to the 1800s in England. At the time, many teams had their own rules, so the game looked very different depending on where it was played. By the 1860s, English soccer clubs began standardizing the rules. This led to the creation of soccer as people know it today.

Germany's Georg Knöpfle, *left*, battles with Uruguay's Pedro Petrone during a 1928 Olympic soccer match.

THROUGHOUT THE YEARS

The first Olympic men's soccer tournament was in 1900. By 1930, the sport had become so popular that it got a stand-alone championship called the World Cup. Men's soccer remained an Olympic sport except for in 1932, when there was a dispute with the organizers. Long limited to amateurs, the Olympic tournament eventually began allowing professionals. But organizers were concerned about having multiple championship competitions. In 1992, they made the Olympics a tournament for players under the age of 23, with three exceptions per team.

Women were long kept out of soccer. That began to change in the 1970s and 1980s. By 1991, women had their own World Cup. The first Olympic women's soccer tournament was in 1996.

Megan Rapinoe and the US women won a bronze medal at the 2020 Olympics.

ICONS

The US women took Olympic soccer by storm. They won the first gold medal in 1996. A women's sports record of 76,481 fans watched the final, a 2–1 win over China in Athens, Georgia. From 2004 through 2012, the Americans won three more gold medals. With three gold medals and one silver, defender Christie Pearce Rampone is the sport's most decorated Olympian. However, when it comes to heroics, it's hard to beat Carli Lloyd, who scored the gold-medal–winning goals in 2008 and 2012.

With its different eligibility rules, the Olympic men's soccer tournament has produced several champions who have never won a World Cup. Among them are Mexico (2012), Nigeria (1996), Cameroon (2000), and Hungary (1952, 1964, 1968). Only Hungary and Great Britain (1900, 1908, 1912) have won three gold medals on the men's side.

Reo Hatate, *center*, of Japan keeps track of the ball while surrounded by players from Spain during the 2020 Olympic semifinal.

SWIMMING

ABOUT THE COMPETITION

Using a predetermined stroke, Olympic swimmers compete in races ranging from 50 to 1,500 meters. The only exceptions are the 10-kilometer marathon events, which are held in open water.

Olympic swimmers use four swimming strokes: the backstroke, breaststroke, butterfly, and freestyle. Technically, freestyle means the swimmer can use any stroke, but in reality everyone uses the crawl because it's the fastest stroke. In addition to individual events, there are also

Team USA's Katie Ledecky won her third consecutive gold medal in the 800-meter freestyle at the 2020 Olympics.

Olympic pools are
50 meters (164 feet) long.

four-person relays in which swimmers from one country race one
after the other. The 2020 Olympics saw the debut of the first mixed
relay, which included two men and two women on each team.

Most races have one defined stroke. In medley races, all four
strokes are used. There are medley races for both individuals
and relays.

ORIGIN

People have been swimming as a means of survival since the beginning of recorded history. As a sport, swim races were first organized during the 1800s in the United Kingdom. Early races used a form of the breaststroke. The front crawl developed later in the century.

OPEN WATER

During the first three Olympics, from 1896 to 1904, all of the swimming events were held in natural bodies of water. The sport moved to pools after that. But in 2008 open-water swimming returned to the Olympics with the inclusion of men's and women's 10,000-meter races. Held in open water, such as a lake or a bay, these events bring added difficulty. Swimmers contend with waves, currents, and other natural conditions. With the races lasting up to two hours, the events are sometimes called marathon swimming.

In 2016, Team USA's Simone Manuel became the first Black woman to win an individual Olympic gold medal in swimming.

THROUGHOUT THE YEARS

Swimming is one of the original Olympic sports. First limited to men, the Olympic swimming program has included women's events since 1912. Early on, all Olympic swimming events were breaststroke or freestyle. Backstroke events were added in 1900. The butterfly debuted in 1956.

ICONS

With so many races, swimming has had no shortage of stars over the years. One of the sport's first true superstars was Johnny Weissmuller. The American won five gold medals between the 1924 and 1928 Olympics, as well as a bronze medal in water polo. He then went on to star in Hollywood films.

Dawn Fraser dominated women's swimming in the middle of the century. The popular Australian won eight total medals from 1956 to 1964. That included three consecutive gold medals in the 100-meter freestyle. No swimmer had done that before.

In 1972, American Mark Spitz set a record that many believed would never be broken. He won seven gold medals in Munich, with each win coming in world record time. Together with his

ARTISTIC SWIMMING

Not all Olympic swimming involves racing. Artistic swimming, formerly called synchronized swimming, began in the 1930s. It first appeared in the Olympics in 1984. In this women-only sport, swimmers perform choreographed routines to music. Although the athletes make their performances look graceful, it can be a grueling sport. Athletes perform lifts, twists, and other maneuvers without touching the bottom of the pool. They must also stay synchronized in their movements. The Olympic program has changed over the years but now includes events for teams of two and eight women. Judges score them in a technical and free routine.

Athletes who compete in artistic swimming must be in sync with their teammates.

performance in 1968, Spitz ended up with 11 total medals, nine of them gold.

Michael Phelps first dove into an Olympic swim race as a 15-year-old in 2000. Four years later, he nearly matched Spitz's record when he won six gold and two bronze medals. In 2008, Phelps finally broke that record—and he did so in stunning fashion. Fans around the world followed along as the Maryland native set about his quest. In just his second race, the 4x100-meter freestyle, teammate Jason Lezak had to mount an epic comeback in the final leg to clinch the gold medal. Then, after dominating his next four races, Phelps faced one of his biggest rivals, Serbia's Milorad Cavic, in the 100-meter butterfly. Coming down to the very end, Phelps edged Cavic by just one hundredth of a second. The next day, a win in the 4x100 medley earned Phelps his eighth gold medal in a single Olympics—a new record. Phelps retired after the 2016 Games with an Olympic record of 28 medals. Twenty-three of them were gold.

Dara Torres didn't have Phelps's total medal count, but her feat at the 2008 Olympics was similarly impressive. At age 41 and competing in her fifth Olympics, the Southern California native won three silver medals. That brought her career total to 12 and made her the oldest medalist in Olympic swimming history.

Katie Ledecky is another standout US swimmer. She competed in the 2012, 2016, and 2020 Olympics, winning ten medals. Seven of those medals were gold and three were silver.

Michael Phelps ended his career at the 2016 Olympics by winning his record 23rd gold medal.

ABOUT THE COMPETITION

Just as the name suggests, table tennis is similar to tennis but played on a table. Players use paddles to hit the ball over a net and onto the opponent's side. If the opponent is unable to safely hit the ball back, a point is earned. In table tennis, singles matches are played up to seven games. Players must reach 11 points and be two points ahead of their opponents to win a game.

Guo Yue, *left*, and Li Xiaoxia of China compete at the 2012 Olympics.

China's Zhang Yining focuses on the ball during a 2008 Olympic match.

ORIGIN

Table tennis is nicknamed "Ping-Pong." It's said to have originated in the late 1800s in England, when upper-class families played after dinner. It eventually spread around the world, becoming particularly popular in China.

THROUGHOUT THE YEARS

The first Olympic table tennis tournaments were held in 1988, with competitions in men's and women's singles and doubles events. Team events replaced doubles in 2008. A mixed doubles event joined the Olympic program at the 2020 Games.

ICONS

China is by far the most successful at table tennis. Zhang Yining is one great player from that country. She won four Olympic gold medals, including two in 2008. She is one of four athletes—all from China—who have won at least four gold medals in the sport.

TAE KWON DO

Great Britain's Jade Jones, *right*, kicks China's Hou Yuzhuo during their 2012 Olympic gold-medal bout.

ABOUT THE COMPETITION

Tae kwon do is a martial art that emphasizes kicking and punching. Athletes earn points for successfully striking their opponents. The more advanced the technique, the more points it earns. A match includes three rounds, each lasting two minutes.

ORIGIN

Tae kwon do is the traditional martial art of Korea. It dates back to around 50 BCE. As a sport, tae kwon do's popularity spread around the Korean Peninsula and then the world during the 1900s.

THROUGHOUT THE YEARS

Tae kwon do was included as a demonstration sport at the 1988 Olympics in Seoul, South Korea. The sport had the same status in 1992. It was finally added as a full medal sport in 2000.

ICONS

No country has won more Olympic tae kwon do medals than South Korea. Hwang Kyung-Seon is the most successful from that country. She won her third medal, and second gold medal, in 2012. That tied her for the most decorated in the sport. Men's competitors Hadi Saei from Iran and Steven Lopez from the United States have also won two gold medals and one bronze medal each.

The proper stance sets up a competitor to effectively attack or defend.

KARATE

Karate is one of the world's most popular martial arts. It was popularized during the 1920s in Japan. The sport was added to the Olympics for the 2020 Games in Tokyo. However, the sport was still seeking a permanent spot on the Olympic program.

TENNIS

ABOUT THE COMPETITION

In tennis, players use rackets to hit a ball over a net. The goal is to send the ball into the opponent's court in such a way that the opponent is unable to successfully hit it back. In a unique scoring system, players try to win games and then sets. The first to claim two sets wins. Olympic tennis includes competitions for men and women in singles and doubles, as well as a mixed doubles event.

Spain's Rafael Nadal has won Olympic gold medals as both a singles and doubles player.

ORIGIN

Although similar games have existed for centuries, modern tennis began in the 1800s in England. It was played on grass and known as lawn tennis. The sport exploded in popularity during the mid-1900s.

THROUGHOUT THE YEARS

Tennis was included in the Olympics from 1896 until 1924. It returned as a full medal sport in 1988.

ICONS

Many of the sport's biggest stars have won Olympic medals. No one has won more than American sisters Serena and Venus Williams. Each have four golds, including three together as doubles partners. In 1988, Germany's Steffi Graf completed "the Golden Slam." She remains the only person to have won all four Grand Slam tournaments plus an Olympic gold

Team USA's Serena Williams has won four Olympic gold medals, tied with her sister Venus for the most ever by a tennis player.

medal in the same year. Great Britain's Andy Murray claimed his first major singles title when he won the 2012 Olympic gold medal on home soil at the famous Wimbledon stadium.

TRACK AND FIELD

ABOUT THE COMPETITION

Track and field includes competitions in running, walking, jumping, and throwing. Also known as athletics, it is the original and, to many, the classic Olympic sport. The running events take place on a track, and athletes race in distances ranging from 100 to 10,000 meters. The only races held away from the track are the racewalks and the marathon, which take place on city streets. Among the track competitions are races with hurdles, a 3,000-meter steeplechase, and relays.

Jumping and throwing competitions take place in the field. These are areas inside and around the track. The long jump and triple jump measure who can jump the farthest. Athletes in the high jump and pole vault aim to get the most height. In the discus, hammer throw, javelin throw, and shot put, athletes compete to see who can send objects farthest in the air.

Two of the most famous track and field events are the decathlon for men and heptathlon for women. In these sports, athletes compete across multiple events—ten for men and seven for women. They are ranked based on their performances in each. The winners are often considered the world's greatest all-around athletes.

RACEWALKING

Not all footraces involve running. The Olympics also feature racewalking. The 20-kilometer event is for both men and women. There's a 50-kilometer race for men too. In these events, athletes must always have one foot in contact with the ground.

Jamaica's Usain Bolt never lost a 100-meter race at the Olympics.

Dutch athlete Fanny Blankers-Koen leaps over the final hurdle in the 80-meter race at the 1948 Olympic Games. She won four gold medals that year.

ORIGIN

Track and field is considered to be the oldest organized sport. When the first ancient Olympics were held in 776 BCE, the first event was a stadium race in which runners sprinted approximately 192 meters (630 feet). Other ancient Olympic track-and-field events included the long jump, discus throw, javelin throw, a race in armor, and the five-event pentathlon. Similar competitions were held across Europe during the next several centuries.

Modern track and field dates back to the mid-1800s in England. The first recorded track meet was held in 1840 in Shropshire, England. By the 1880s, similar events were held in the United States and other countries.

THROUGHOUT THE YEARS

Track and field has been part of the modern Olympics since 1896. The first competition had just 12 events, and all of them were limited to men. The track program at the 2020 Olympics included 48 events—24 for men, 23 for women, and one mixed. Achieving that balance took many years. The first women's events were added in 1928. However, after some of the runners appeared exhausted following the 800-meter run, organizers banned women's events longer than 200 meters (656 feet). It wasn't until 1960 that the women's 800-meter event returned. A women's marathon was added in 1984. More women's events continued to be added in the years that followed.

The women who ran the 1984 Olympic marathon proved that women were capable of endurance running.

ICONS

In 1896, James Connolly left his home in Boston, Massachusetts, and boarded a boat to Europe. In Greece, he became the first modern Olympic champion after winning the event now known as the triple jump.

Jesse Owens's feats at the 1936 Olympics in Berlin became legendary. The US star won the 100-, 200-, and 4x100-meter races, as well as the long jump. He set multiple records in the process. Notably, Owens, who was Black, accomplished all of this against a backdrop of racism both at home and in Nazi Germany.

Jamaica's Usain Bolt later captivated the world with his stunning sprinting performances. He won gold medals in the 100-, 200-, and 4x100-meter in 2008, 2012, and 2016. However, a relay medal was later taken away because one of his teammates had used banned performance-enhancing drugs.

For a long time, women had to prove to male organizers that they belonged on the Olympic track. Sprinter Fanny Blankers-Koen of the Netherlands won four gold

Jesse Owens became an Olympic legend for thriving in the face of adversity at the 1936 Olympic Games in Berlin.

American Joan Benoit runs in the marathon at the 1984 Olympic Games in Los Angeles.

medals in 1948. As a mother of two, she helped change perceptions of what women could do. In 1984, Team USA's Joan Benoit showed women could handle the most grueling distance race when she cruised to victory in the first Olympic women's marathon. That same year, American Jackie Joyner-Kersee made her Olympic debut in the heptathlon. Over her career she won six medals, three of them gold, between the heptathlon and long jump. She's recognized as one of the greatest all-around athletes ever.

The Olympics have featured many other epic performances. In 1968, American Bob Beamon broke the world record in long jump by nearly 0.6 meters (2 feet). Fellow American Al Oerter won the discus gold medal that year. That made him the first track athlete to win the same event four times in a row. Twenty years later, US sprinter Florence Griffith Joyner won three gold medals and a silver. She nearly broke her own world record in the 100-meter, and she twice set a new world record in the 200-meter. Both still stood at the time of the 2020 Olympics.

Triathlon is a popular spectator sport at the Olympics. Part of the race is often open to the public.

ABOUT THE COMPETITION

The triathlon is an endurance race. It combines three sports that happen one after another. In the Olympics, athletes begin with a 1,500-meter (4,921 foot) swim. Then they have to do a 40-kilometer (25 mile) bike ride. Athletes end with a 10-kilometer (6.2 mile) run. Whoever crosses the finish line first is the winner.

ORIGIN

In the 1970s, the first triathlon was held in San Diego, California. Before long, triathlons were taking place around the world.

THROUGHOUT THE YEARS

The triathlon was added to the Olympics in 2000. There were competitions for both men and women. A mixed relay featuring teams of two men and two women from a single country was added for the 2020 Olympics.

ICONS

Gwen Jorgensen had been a distance runner and swimmer. She had never ridden a road bike before deciding to try a triathlon. Jorgensen proved to be a fast learner. She made the Olympic team in 2012. She then dominated the sport before winning the Olympic gold medal in 2016. Great Britain's Jonny Brownlee is the most decorated Olympic triathlete, with a medal of every color. His brother Alistair Brownlee is the sport's only two-time gold medalist, having won in 2012 and 2016.

Team USA's Gwen Jorgensen, *right*, was a dominant runner, which helped her win the gold in 2016.

VOLLEYBALL

ABOUT THE COMPETITION

In volleyball, a team works together to send a ball over a net and onto the opponent's court. At the same time, the team tries to prevent the opponent from grounding the ball on its court. Players may use only their hands and arms to touch the ball. Holding the ball is not allowed.

In the Olympics, there are two volleyball competitions: beach and indoor. In both versions, teams can hit the ball three times before sending it over the net. However, there are some key differences between the two competitions. Indoor volleyball teams have six players on the court at a time. Their games are played in a gym. Beach volleyball teams are made up of just two players. Their court is made of sand. Scoring in the two games in similar, though indoor games are best-of-five sets while beach plays best-of-three sets.

Jordan Larson, *center*, led the US women's indoor volleyball team to its first Olympic gold medal in the 2020 Games.

Team USA's Phil Dalhausser competed in beach volleyball at four Olympics, winning a gold medal in 2008.

ORIGIN

In 1895, American William G. Morgan came up with the idea for volleyball, which was originally called mintonette. Indoor volleyball began spreading around the world. It became more competitive and athletically grueling over the years.

By the 1920s, people in Santa Monica, California, had taken the game outside to the beach as well. Competitive beach volleyball teams began to emerge in the 1980s. The sport quickly grew from there.

THROUGHOUT THE YEARS

Indoor volleyball was added to the Olympics in 1964. Unlike the other traditional team sports contested there—basketball, field hockey, soccer, and water polo—volleyball had competitions for both men and women. Beach volleyball was added to the Olympics in 1996.

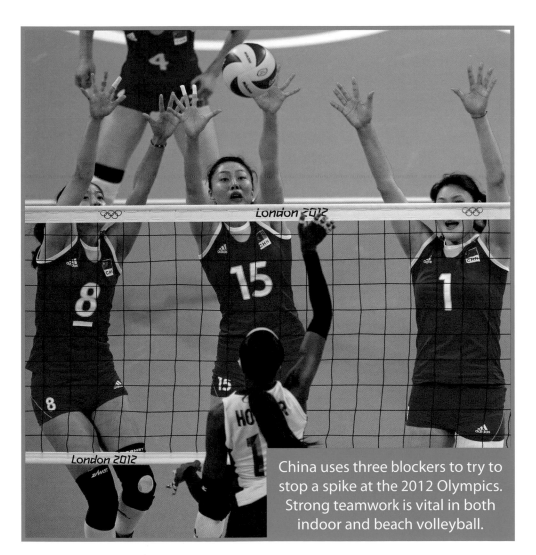

China uses three blockers to try to stop a spike at the 2012 Olympics. Strong teamwork is vital in both indoor and beach volleyball.

ICONS

Japan's women's volleyball team at the 1964 Olympics became famous for its intensity. The players did clerical work at a company during the day. Then they battled through extreme training sessions until midnight. Players such as captain Masae Kasai learned to dive and roll to keep the ball in play. It proved to be an effective tactic. The team went on to defeat the Soviet Union to win the sport's first Olympic gold medal.

No one team has dominated indoor volleyball. On the women's side, the Soviet Union won four gold medals. Both China and Cuba have won three each. Cuba's came all in a row, in 1992, 1996, and 2000. Regla Bell, Marlenis Costa, Mireya Luis, and Regla Torres were members of all three teams.

It's a similar story on the men's side. Russia won the 2012 gold medal to go along with three won by the former Soviet Union. Brazil and the United States have each won three gold medals. Karch Kiraly was a star for two of those US teams, in 1984 and 1988. Then he switched to beach volleyball and won a third gold medal in 1996. Many consider him to be the sport's all-time greatest player.

When it comes to beach volleyball, nobody can match the partnership of Americans Kerri Walsh Jennings and Misty May-Treanor. Both made their Olympic debuts in 2000, although Walsh Jennings was playing indoor volleyball and May-Treanor had a different partner. Upon joining forces, they went on to win consecutive gold medals in 2004, 2008, and 2012. They won all 21 of their Olympic matches together. In 43 Olympic sets, the duo won 42 of them. May-Treanor retired after that, but Walsh Jennings went on to compete in a fifth Olympics. She took home a bronze medal in 2016 with her new partner, April Ross.

Kerri Walsh Jennings, *right*, and US teammate Misty May-Treanor, *left*, won their third Olympic gold medal together in 2012.

WATER POLO

ABOUT THE COMPETITION

Water polo is a rugged team sport where athletes swimming in a pool try to send a ball into their opponent's goal. Once a team gains possession, it must shoot within 30 seconds. If it fails to do so, the opponent takes over. Players must constantly tread water to stay afloat, and physical contact is common. A game lasts 32 minutes. It's divided into four equal quarters.

ORIGIN

The first water polo games were played in the United Kingdom during the 1870s. Not long after, a similar sport emerged in the United States. The American game featured a semi-inflated ball and was very aggressive. In 1914, the United States decided to play the faster-paced European version, which is the standard today.

Australia's Abby Andrews, *center*, attempts to block a pass during the 2020 Olympics.

THROUGHOUT THE YEARS

Men's water polo has been part of the Olympics since 1900. That was the first time traditional team sports were included in the Games. Despite the sport's rich history on the men's side, women's water polo didn't become an Olympic event until 2000.

In water polo, each team has seven active players.

Players from Hungary's men's team show off their gold medals in 2008.

ICONS

Australia, Italy, and then the Netherlands won the first three Olympic women's water polo gold medals. The United States took over after that. Team USA won its first gold medal in 2012. In the years that followed, it continued to win every major competition in the sport—including the 2016 and 2020 gold medals. Two players were members of all three US Olympic teams: Maggie Steffens and Melissa Seidemann. Ashleigh Johnson, a dominant goalie, starred on the latter two gold-medal teams.

On the men's side, Great Britain dominated the early Olympic years. However, no country can compare to Hungary. The Hungarians have won a record nine gold medals in water polo. Between 1932 and 1980, the team never missed the podium. It later won three in a row from 2000 to 2008.

WEIGHT LIFTING

ABOUT THE COMPETITION

Weight lifters compete to see who can lift the heaviest combined weight over two types of lifts. During a snatch, the lifter brings the weight above his or her head in one motion. In a clean and jerk, the lifter brings the weight to the chest, then presses the bar above the head. Competitors have three attempts at each. Their best lifts in each style are added together to determine a total weight.

ORIGIN

Tests of power and strength date back to ancient Egypt and Greece. However, competitive weight lifting as we know it today originated in the 1800s.

In the Olympics, men compete in eight different weight classes. Women have seven classes.

THROUGHOUT THE YEARS

Weight lifting has been featured at nearly every Olympics since the first in 1896, although early competitions used different formats. Weight classes were added in 1920. The modern format has been in place since 1976. It was not until 2000 that a women's event was included.

Athletes lift plates that range in size. The plates are color-coded.

ICONS

Turkey's Halil Mutlu was in an elite class. He could lift three times his body weight. In 2004, he tied the record by winning his third weight lifting gold medal. Among the three others to achieve that feat was his fellow countryman Naim Süleymanoğlu, who earned his third gold medal in 1996.

China has emerged as a weight lifting power. In 2008, Chen Yanqing won her second gold medal. She broke her own Olympic record in the process.

WRESTLING

Helen Maroulis celebrates after winning a gold medal at the 2016 Olympics.

ABOUT THE COMPETITION

In wrestling, two competitors use grappling techniques to try to pin each other's shoulder to the mat. Wrestlers also earn points for certain actions, such as a takedown or throw. If neither wrestler pins their opponent, the person with the most points wins.

Two forms of wrestling are included in the Olympics. In Greco-Roman, athletes are limited to using their upper bodies. Freestyle wrestlers are allowed to use their legs. Athletes are grouped together in weight classes to ensure competitors are of similar sizes.

ORIGINS

Wrestling is considered the world's oldest sport. The earliest known references to wrestling come from 3000 BCE in Babylonia and Egypt. However, wrestling also existed in other areas, including in ancient China and India. Greco-Roman and freestyle emerged as the most popular wrestling styles in the late 1800s.

Greco-Roman wrestlers must try to take down their opponents using only their upper bodies.

THROUGHOUT THE YEARS

When choosing the sports for the first modern Olympics, organizers included Greco-Roman wrestling. They believed it created a link between the ancient and modern Games. Freestyle wrestling, which was more popular in the United States, was included in 1904. Both Greco-Roman and freestyle have been seen in every Olympics since 1920. However, competition was limited to men until 2004, when women's freestyle was added.

ICONS

Known as "the Russian Bear," Aleksandr Karelin dominated Greco-Roman wrestling for a generation. Competing in the super heavyweight class, Karelin didn't just win matches—he dominated them. He used his tremendous power to win Olympic gold medals in 1988, 1992, and 1996. Most people were certain Karelin would win one more in 2000. However, in a stunning upset, he fell to American Rulon Gardner in the gold-medal match. That marked Karelin's first loss in 13 years. Two decades later, Mijaín López of Cuba became the first man to win four Olympic gold medals in the sport. The Greco-Roman super heavyweight won every title from 2008 to 2020.

Women got a later start in Olympic wrestling, but two Japanese women made up for lost time. Kaori Icho won her fourth consecutive gold medal in 2016. Saori Yoshida nearly matched that feat one day later. In a rematch of the 2012 world championships final, Yoshida faced US wrestler Helen Maroulis. Yoshida had dominated their 2012 fight. This time, however, Maroulis fought back from an early deficit to score a takedown. She won Team USA's first Olympic gold medal in women's wrestling.

Russia's Aleksandr Karelin, *left*, finally met his match against Rulon Gardner of the United States in the 2000 Olympics.

ADDITIONAL SPORTS

The Olympic programs are always changing. Sometimes entire sports are added or removed. For the 2020 Olympics in Tokyo, the IOC added some new sports. Baseball/softball and karate were included for just the Tokyo Games. Skateboarding, sport climbing, and surfing were contested in Tokyo and were also planned for the 2024 program, along with competitive break dancing.

BASEBALL/SOFTBALL

Men's baseball came to the Olympics in 1992. Women's softball joined in 1996. Both were dropped following the 2008 Games. However, the IOC decided to combine them as separate disciplines within a single sport for the 2020 Games.

Japan beat Team USA in the 2008 and 2020, *pictured*, softball gold-medal games.

BREAKING

Breaking is also known as break dancing. Athletes compete one-on-one. They are judged for their exciting flips, spins, and other moves. The IOC voted to include this sport for the first time in 2024.

KARATE

Karate is a Japanese martial art. It has competitions in kumite, which is one-on-one combat, and kata, which is a choreographed performance.

SKATEBOARDING

Skateboarders ride in park competitions held in hollowed-out courses. They also compete in street events. These courses have elements mimicking ordinary streets.

Japan's Sakura Yosozumi won gold in women's park skateboarding at the 2020 Games.

SPORT CLIMBING

In sport climbing, athletes compete in a combined event featuring three styles of climbing: bouldering, lead climbing, and speed.

SURFING

The Olympic surfing competition features riders who compete head-to-head with each other. They earn points for their maneuvers.

WINTER SPORTS

Figure skating events were held at the 1908 Olympic Games. In 1920, the Olympics included both figure skating and ice hockey. The popularity of those events led the IOC to create a separate event just for winter sports. So in 1924, a gathering for winter sports competitions was held in Chamonix, France. Although it went by a different name at the time, the event is now considered the first Olympic Winter Games.

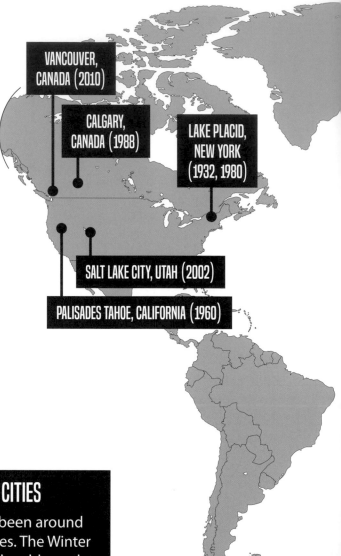

VANCOUVER, CANADA (2010)

CALGARY, CANADA (1988)

LAKE PLACID, NEW YORK (1932, 1980)

SALT LAKE CITY, UTAH (2002)

PALISADES TAHOE, CALIFORNIA (1960)

WINTER GAMES HOST CITIES

The Winter Games haven't been around as long as the Summer Games. The Winter Games take place in cities with cold weather and nearby mountains.

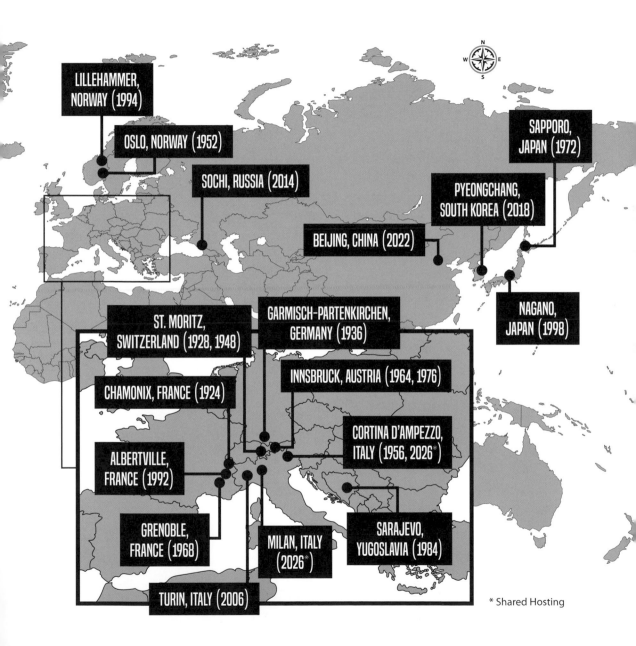

LILLEHAMMER, NORWAY (1994)

OSLO, NORWAY (1952)

SOCHI, RUSSIA (2014)

SAPPORO, JAPAN (1972)

PYEONGCHANG, SOUTH KOREA (2018)

BEIJING, CHINA (2022)

NAGANO, JAPAN (1998)

ST. MORITZ, SWITZERLAND (1928, 1948)

GARMISCH-PARTENKIRCHEN, GERMANY (1936)

CHAMONIX, FRANCE (1924)

INNSBRUCK, AUSTRIA (1964, 1976)

CORTINA D'AMPEZZO, ITALY (1956, 2026*)

ALBERTVILLE, FRANCE (1992)

GRENOBLE, FRANCE (1968)

MILAN, ITALY (2026*)

SARAJEVO, YUGOSLAVIA (1984)

TURIN, ITALY (2006)

* Shared Hosting

ALPINE SKIING

ABOUT THE COMPETITION

Alpine skiing is also called downhill skiing. In these races, skiers try to get from the top of a hill to the bottom as quickly as possible. During the races, skiers must follow paths between or around gates. If skiers get off course, they are disqualified.

There are five individual alpine skiing races. Slalom and giant slalom are considered the technical events. They are shorter races, and the gates are placed closer together. In both, skiers complete two runs. The downhill is the longest and straightest course. That makes it the fastest race, with skiers moving as fast as 90 miles per hour (145 kmh). The other speed event is the super giant slalom, known as super-G. It has elements from both the giant slalom and downhill.

There is also an alpine combined event. In this competition, a skier completes a slalom and a downhill run. The times from both races are added together.

Austria's Hermann Maier won gold medals in the super-G and giant slalom at the 1998 Olympic Winter Games.

Italy's Alberto Tomba races the slalom during the 1988 Olympic Winter Games in Calgary.

ORIGIN

People have used some form of skis to move around on the snow since ancient times. Modern cross-country skiing developed during the 1800s in Norway. The skis used there eventually spread to mainland Europe. People began adapting the skis to use on steep mountain slopes, such as the Alps, which is how the sport got its name.

The first alpine ski race was a slalom held in 1922 in Switzerland. One year later, a combined slalom and downhill event took place. The sport grew from there, though it wasn't popular enough to be included in the first Winter Olympics in 1924.

THROUGHOUT THE YEARS

Alpine skiing is one of the rare Olympic sports that has always had the same events for both men and women. It debuted in the Olympics in 1936, with men's and women's alpine combined competitions. Individual downhill and slalom races were added in 1948, followed by the giant slalom in 1952. Super-G made its Olympic debut in 1988.

In 2018, the Olympic alpine program grew with the addition of a mixed team event. Each round features four parallel slalom races. In these races, two men and two women from one country go head-to-head with counterparts from another country.

Picabo Street of the United States races in the super-G at the 1998 Games.

ICONS

Andrea Mead Lawrence was one of the first stars of Olympic alpine skiing. The American won both the slalom and giant slalom at the 1952 Olympics. That made her the first to claim two alpine gold medals in one Olympics.

No alpine skier has won more Olympic medals than Kjetil André Aamodt of Norway. He won eight between 1992 and 2006, including four golds. Most impressively, his medals came in four of the five events, falling short only in slalom. Janica Kostelić of Croatia leads all women in this sport with six medals. Three of her four golds came in 2002. She also won a silver medal that year. That made her the first in the sport to win four medals in one Olympics. Only two other skiers have won three gold medals in one Olympics. Austria's Toni Sailer achieved this in 1956. France's Jean-Claude Killy did it in 1968.

Sweden's Ingemar Stenmark and Italy's Alberto Tomba were great rivals in the technical events during the 1980s. Tomba won three gold medals and two silver medals. Stenmark won two golds and a bronze. However, Stenmark is recognized as the sport's greatest technical skier for his results outside of the Olympics. That's a title that could be passed on to Mikaela Shiffrin. The American became the youngest slalom gold medalist ever at age 18 in 2014. Four years later, she won giant slalom and took home a silver medal in alpine combined.

Mikaela Shiffrin of Team USA emerged as alpine skiing's next great star during the 2014 Olympics.

ABOUT THE COMPETITION

The biathlon competition involves two sports: cross-country skiing and rifle shooting. In a biathlon race, skiers make intermittent stops to shoot at targets. For each target they miss, skiers are penalized either by added time or by having to ski an extra lap.

ORIGIN

The concept of skiing and shooting developed in Scandinavia. People there combined the two activities as a means of survival. Biathlon as a sport began in the 1700s, although the first modern biathlon was held in 1912 in Norway.

WINTER PENTATHLON

Before biathlon was added to the Olympics, officials wanted a winter version of the modern pentathlon. As a result, a winter pentathlon was held as a demonstration sport in 1948. It included a cross-country ski race and a downhill ski race. It also had competitions in fencing, shooting, and horse jumping.

The strenuous racing in biathlon raises the athletes' heart rates, which makes it more difficult to shoot accurately.

A mass start biathlon event was added to the Olympics in 2006. The Olympic program also includes sprint, pursuit, individual, and relay races.

THROUGHOUT THE YEARS

After appearing in three Winter Games as a demonstration sport, men's biathlon was officially added to the Olympics in 1960. A women's event followed in 1992. At first consisting of only one individual race and one relay, the Olympic biathlon has expanded to include five races for men and women, plus a mixed relay.

ICONS

Norway's Ole Einar Bjørndalen didn't win any medals at his first Olympics in 1994. But over the next five Winter Games, he won 13 medals, eight of which were gold. That made him the most decorated man in the Winter Olympics at the time. Germany's Uschi Disl leads all women in this sport. She has nine Olympic biathlon medals, two of them gold. She earned them between 1992 and 2006.

BOBSLED

ABOUT THE COMPETITION

Bobsled is also called bobsleigh. It's a sport in which athletes race a heavy sled down a banked, ice-covered track. Each sled is equipped with steel runners that slide on the ice. In the Olympics, there are races for one-, two-, and four-person sleds.

ORIGIN

The first bobsled races took place in the 1860s in Switzerland. By 1900, bobsledding had become a popular activity for wealthy tourists.

Germany's four-man bobsled team raced its way to gold in the 2018 Winter Games.

124

Bobsledders can reach high speeds. Some get up to around 80 miles per hour (129 kmh).

THROUGHOUT THE YEARS

Men's bobsled events have been part of the Olympics since the first Winter Games in 1924. Men have competed in two- and four-man events since 1932. A two-woman event made its Olympic debut in 2002. A solo women's event, called the monobob, was added for the 2022 Winter Games.

ICONS

In 2002, Americans Jill Bakken and Vonetta Flowers won the first gold medal in women's bobsled. In doing so, Flowers also became the first Black athlete to win a gold medal in the Winter Games.

Eight years later, in the men's competition, US pilot Steven Holcomb drove his four-man sled nicknamed "Night Train" to victory. It marked Team USA's first gold medal in the event since 1948. Four years later, he drove two- and four-man sleds to silver medals.

CURLING

The round curling stone has a handle on the top and a concaved bottom.

ABOUT THE COMPETITION

In curling, teams slide heavy granite stones across the ice. The goal is to end each round with the stones closest to a target. Traditional teams have four people. Doubles teams have just two. One person slides the stone while the teammates use brooms to sweep the ice. This creates a smoother path for the stone.

ORIGIN

Although a similar game was played on frozen ponds in the Netherlands, Scotland is considered the home of curling. The game has been played there since the 1500s. The rules and organization of the modern game developed there in the 1800s.

THROUGHOUT THE YEARS

Men's curling was included in the 1924 Winter Games. Then it appeared a handful of other times as a demonstration sport. Finally, in 1998, men's and women's curling joined the Olympic program. A mixed doubles event debuted in 2018.

ICONS

Canada is the most successful Olympic curling country with 11 medals, six of which are gold. John Morris and Kaitlyn Lawes each have two gold medals. Among US curlers, John Shuster stands alone. He won a bronze medal in 2006. Then, as the leader, his teams struggled in 2010 and 2014. However, in 2018 his US team made a thrilling comeback to win gold.

Strategy is a major part of curling, with athletes having to think several moves ahead.

FIGURE SKATING

ABOUT THE COMPETITION

In figure skating, athletes wearing ice skates perform routines to music on a large sheet of ice. There are competitions for men, women, and pairs of one man and one woman. In addition, teams of one man and one woman compete in ice dancing.

Dorothy Hamill took home figure skating gold for the United States in 1976.

Canada's Tessa Virtue and Scott Moir are the most decorated Olympic figure skaters, with a total of five medals.

In each discipline, a competition includes a short program and a long program, or free skate. Skaters must perform certain moves in a short program. There are fewer requirements for the long program, so skaters have more freedom in how they choreograph their performances.

The singles and pairs competitions emphasize elegance and athleticism. Each performance includes elements such as spins, step sequences, and high-flying jumps. In pairs, the skaters also do lifts, throw jumps, and other elements that must be done in unison. Ice dance is different from the other events. Teams must perform dance patterns to the music. It's similar to ballroom dancing but on ice. Jumps and spins are not allowed.

Judges grade performances based on technical elements and overall presentation. The presentation includes elements such as skating, transitions, and interpretation of the music.

ORIGIN

People in the Netherlands were using ice skates to get around on the country's frozen canals as early as the 1200s. Eventually, skates became popular for recreation too. By the mid-1700s, people in Great Britain were using their skates to trace figures onto ice. This is how figure skating got its name.

Two important developments helped shape the sport as we know it today. In 1850, steel blades were introduced. These allowed skaters to perform more complex movements. Shortly after, American ballet master Jackson Haines incorporated music and dance into the sport. These changes helped make figure skating more athletic and artistic.

THROUGHOUT THE YEARS

Figure skating is the oldest winter sport in the Olympics. Competitions were held in 1908 and 1920—before the Winter Games even existed. Men's, women's, and pairs events have been part of every Winter Games since the first one in 1924. Ice dance was added to the program in 1972. As one of the most popular winter sports, Olympic figure skating grew again in 2014 with the addition of a team competition.

One of the biggest changes in Olympic figure skating came before the 1992 Winter Games. At that time, the sport ended compulsory figures. This round of competition required skaters to trace patterns, such as circles, on the ice. However, many found compulsory figures to be boring compared with the freestyle skating in the short and long programs.

Yuna Kim of South Korea dazzled fans at the 2010 Winter Games with her record-setting performance in the free skate.

ICONS

Perhaps no skater changed the sport as much as Dick Button did. At the 1948 Olympics, the American star became the first person to land the difficult double axel jump in competition. Four years later, he became the first to land a triple jump in competition. Button won gold medals both years, and his new jumps and spins helped revolutionize the sport. Other male stars followed Button, but it wasn't until Japan's Yuzuru Hanyu that another man defended his Olympic title. Showcasing four-rotation quad jumps, Hanyu won gold in 2014 and 2018.

Sonja Henie was another iconic Olympic figure skater. After debuting in the 1924 Winter Games at age 11, the Norwegian skater captivated audiences with her gold-medal performances in 1928, 1932, and 1936. Henie combined elements of ballet with exquisite spinning. After her Olympic career, Henie's popularity grew. She performed in ice shows and in Hollywood movies.

Henie's stardom helped grow the sport around the world. It also set a blueprint that many others would follow. Figure skating became one of the most popular winter Olympic sports. Gold medalists such as Americans Carol Heiss (1960), Peggy Fleming (1968), Dorothy Hamill (1976), Kristi Yamaguchi (1992), Tara Lipinski (1998), and Sarah Hughes (2002) became big stars. East Germany's Katarina Witt became the only woman besides Henie to successfully defend her Olympic gold medal when she won in 1984 and 1988. In 2010,

US figure skater Dick Button changed figure skating with his high-flying jumps.

South Korea's Yuna Kim won her country's first figure skating gold medal with a mesmerizing performance.

Russia, including the former Soviet Union, has traditionally dominated pairs skating. Irina Rodnina became the only pairs skater to win three gold medals, doing so in 1972 with Aleksey Ulanov and in 1976 and 1980 with Aleksandr Zaytsev. After years of Soviet and Russian dominance in ice dance, the Canadian team of Tessa Virtue and Scott Moir won two gold medals and a silver between 2010 and 2018. They also won a gold and silver in the team competition.

Katarina Witt performs in the women's free skate at the 1988 Winter Olympics in Calgary.

Team USA's Sarah Hughes surprised many people when she won the women's gold medal on home ice in 2002.

ABOUT THE COMPETITION

Freestyle skiing has several events. Most of them involve thrilling tricks rather than timed races. Aerials and moguls are the oldest forms of freestyle skiing in the Olympics. In aerials, skiers launch themselves off massive jumps and perform different flips and twists before landing on the snow. Moguls skiers must navigate large bumps, called moguls, on steep courses while also performing tricks off two jumps. They are judged for their speeds, techniques, and tricks. Freestyle skiing also includes four other events: big air, half-pipe, ski cross, and slopestyle.

ORIGIN

People began performing tricks and stunts on skis during the 1930s. In 1971, skiers took part in a competition in which they showed off their skills while going down a mogul hill. Around the same time, aerials competitions began gaining popularity. Both styles became internationally recognized under the name freestyle skiing in 1979.

Belarus's Alla Tsuper shows off her aerial skills during the 2014 Winter Games.

THROUGHOUT THE YEARS

Freestyle skiing debuted as an Olympic demonstration sport in 1988. Men's and women's moguls events were officially added to the Games in 1992. The next Winter Games included men's and women's aerials. That program remained intact until the 2010s, when the other events were added.

France's Perrine Laffont won a gold medal in the 2018 women's moguls event.

ICONS

There's not much snow in Puerto Rico, where Jonny Moseley was born. Once he experienced skiing, though, he was hooked. Moseley and his family moved to California, and he began training to become a groundbreaking moguls skier. After just missing out on the 1994 Games, Moseley competed in his first Olympics in 1998. He won a gold medal with help from his signature trick, a 360 mute grab nicknamed the "Iron Cross." His aggressive skiing and innovative tricks helped him become a big star in the growing sport.

Jonny Moseley shows off his gold medal after winning the freestyle moguls event at the 1998 Games.

Alisa Camplin was already an accomplished sailor and gymnast when an aerials coach noticed her natural athletic ability. He thought she'd do well in freestyle skiing. Already 19 years old and not knowing how to ski, she decided to give it a shot. In 2002, at age 27, Camplin made her first Olympic team. Performing a pair of triple-twisting, double backflip jumps, she went on to win Australia's first Olympic skiing gold medal. Four years later, she added a bronze medal.

ABOUT THE COMPETITION

Ice hockey involves teams of players who use sticks to try to send a puck into their opponent's goal. The concept is much the same as field hockey, with the most obvious difference being that the winter sport is played on a sheet of ice, so players wear skates to move around. In the Olympics, ice hockey games consist of three 20-minute periods. At full strength, teams have six players on the ice at a time. Except for in special circumstances, one of those players is a goalie. Ice hockey is a fast-paced sport. Players can substitute in and out of the game on the fly.

Canada's Sidney Crosby slips the puck past Team USA's goalie during overtime in the 2010 Olympic men's gold-medal game.

ORIGIN

Ice hockey originated in Canada during the mid-1800s. It was likely inspired by similar stick-based games, including those played by the Mi'kmaq people in Nova Scotia. The first formal rules of the sport were written in 1879 by students in Montreal. Ice hockey soon spread to the United States and later to Europe.

Hayley Wickenheiser led Canada to four gold medals in her five Olympics.

US winger Weldon Olson, *left*, battles for the puck with Czechoslovakian winger Miroslav Vlach in the opening game in 1960.

THROUGHOUT THE YEARS

The first Olympic ice hockey tournament took place in 1920, before the Winter Games existed. In fact, the popularity of figure skating and ice hockey at those Olympics helped push the IOC to create the Winter Games in 1924. A men's tournament has been included ever since.

For much of its history, hockey was limited to men. That began to change in the late 1980s. The first women's world championship event was held in 1990. By 1998, women's ice hockey had grown large enough that it was added to the Olympics.

Team USA's Jennifer Schmidgall, *top*, and Canada's Therese Brisson get physical at the 1998 Olympic Winter Games in Nagano, Japan.

ICONS

Perhaps unsurprisingly, Canada dominated the early years of Olympic men's hockey. It won six of the first seven gold medals. However, the Soviet Union then emerged as the global force in the sport. Playing a style that was more about finesse than physicality, the Soviet Union (or Unified Team of former Soviet athletes) won all but two of the ten gold medals awarded between 1956 and 1992.

The two exceptions in that streak were iconic US teams. In 1960, an underdog US squad upset Canada and the Soviet Union on the way to the country's first gold medal in hockey. Twenty years later, the US team—made up of mostly college players—was again considered an underdog, especially after losing 10–3 to the Soviet Union just before the Olympics. However, in a rematch during the final round of the Olympics, Team USA never quit. Down 1–0, then 2–1, then 3–2, the Americans tied it up. Captain Mike Eruzione put the team ahead midway through the third period. Goalie Jim Craig held off a flurry of Soviet chances to secure the win. Then Team USA beat Finland in its final game to clinch the gold medal. The US win is known as the "Miracle on Ice."

Team USA celebrates after beating the Soviet Union at the 1980 Olympic Winter Games in Lake Placid, New York.

After a 50-year gap, Canada finally regained the men's gold medal in 2002. However, the most memorable win might have come eight years later. Playing on home ice in Vancouver, rising star Sidney Crosby scored the overtime winner to secure the gold medal in a tense contest with Team USA.

By the time women's hockey made its Olympic debut in 1998, Canada and the United States had established themselves as the sport's powers. They had met in the title game of every previous world championship, with Canada winning each time. At the Olympics, however, Team USA came back from a 4–1 deficit to beat Canada 7–4 in the group stage. Three days later, in a rematch for the gold medal, American Sandra Whyte had two assists before scoring an empty net goal in a 3–1 win.

Canada regained its top position after that, winning each of the next four gold medals. Three of those gold-medal wins came against Team USA. Marie-Philip Poulin scored the winning goal in both the 2010 and 2014 finals.

Team USA finally got its revenge when the fierce rivals met again in the thrilling 2018 gold-medal game. With Canada leading 2–1 late, American Monique Lamoureux sent in the game-tying goal. Then her twin sister Jocelyne Lamoureux-Davidson scored the game-winning goal in a shoot-out.

US players Michelle Picard (23) and Kelli Stack (16) battle with Canada's Caroline Ouellette during the 2014 Olympic gold-medal game.

LUGE

ABOUT THE COMPETITION

Luge is a sliding sport. Athletes lie on their backs while guiding sleds down banked, ice-covered tracks. Olympic luge includes singles events for men and women. A doubles event is open to anyone. There is also a mixed relay in which a woman, a man, and a doubles team from one country race back-to-back for a combined time.

Luge is the fastest winter sport. Athletes can reach up to 90 miles per hour (145 kmh).

ORIGIN

Luge began during the 1500s in Switzerland. The first dedicated luge tracks were built 300 years later at Swiss resorts. Although races were held in the 1800s, the sport didn't become formally organized until the 1950s.

THROUGHOUT THE YEARS

Men's, women's, and doubles luge was added to the Olympics for the 1964 Winter Games. The mixed team relay was added in 2014.

ICONS

German athletes have won more than half of all Olympic luge medals. Natalie Geisenberger is the most decorated luger with four gold medals and a bronze. She won women's and relay golds in 2014 and 2018. Her relay teammates, doubles partners Tobias Arlt and Tobias Wendl, matched that. Felix Loch, meanwhile, won back-to-back men's golds in 2010 and 2014.

Germany has won more Olympic luge medals than any other country, including the gold medal in the 2018 team relay.

NORDIC SKIING

ABOUT THE COMPETITION

Nordic skiing includes several events that use skis in which the heel is not connected to the binding. The Nordic skiing disciplines in the Olympics are cross-country skiing, ski jumping, and Nordic combined.

In cross-country skiing, athletes race across different types of terrain rather than traveling only downhill. There are two types of cross-country skiing techniques. In the classic technique, skiers propel themselves by moving their skis forward and backward, as if they're walking. The freestyle technique looks more like ice skating, which is why it's sometimes called skate skiing. In the Olympics, events range from short sprint distances to as long as 30-kilometer races for women and 50-kilometer races for men.

American Todd Lodwick competes in ski jump during the Nordic combined at the 2010 Olympics.

In ski jumping, athletes slide down large ramps. Then they fly through the air as far as they can. Their performances are graded for both distance and form.

Nordic combined involves competition in both ski jumping and cross-country skiing. Athletes begin by ski jumping. Their results determine the order in which they start a 10-kilometer cross-country race, with the best jumper starting first. The first person to reach the finish line wins. There are two individual events and one team event in the Olympics.

ORIGINS

Skis have been used since ancient times as a way to get around in the snow. Nordic skiing as people know it today originated in the 1800s in Norway. The first known cross-country skiing race was held in 1842. Soon after, in 1866, the first ski jumping competition was held in Norway. By the end of the century, Nordic combined had become a popular sport in that country.

Billy Demong, *front*, and Johnny Spillane helped Team USA win a silver medal in the Nordic combined team event in 2010, marking the country's first Olympic medal in the sport.

THROUGHOUT THE YEARS

All three Nordic disciplines have been part of the Olympics since the first Winter Games in 1924. Originally, Nordic combined was seen as the most prestigious event. A team event was added in 1988. The sport took its current Olympic format in 2010.

A second ski jumping competition was added in 1964. Then a team event first took place in 1988. However, it wasn't until 2014 that a women's ski jumping event was included.

A major change in cross-country skiing occurred in the 1970s, when American Bill Koch developed a skating-like technique. This would later become freestyle. Now all events are designated as either classic or freestyle. Over the years, the sport has also switched from time trials to now mostly mass start races.

In 2018, Jessie Diggins, *left*, celebrates after winning the team sprint for Team USA's first gold medal in cross-country skiing.

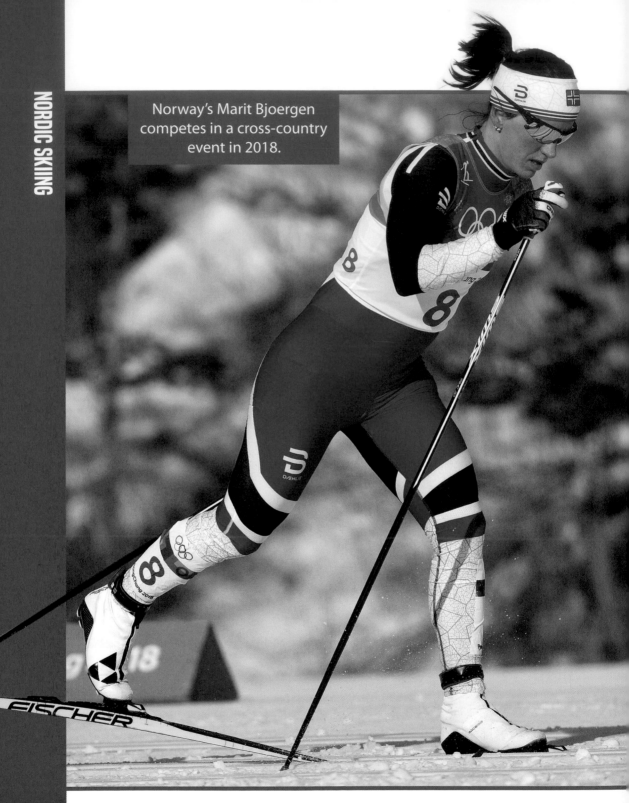

Norway's Marit Bjoergen competes in a cross-country event in 2018.

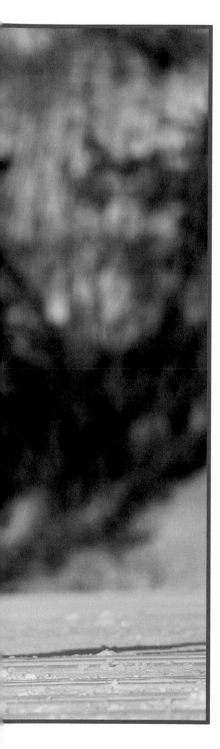

ICONS

Unsurprisingly, Norway and the other Nordic countries have dominated cross-country skiing. Two of the most decorated winter Olympians are Norwegian cross-country skiers. Marit Bjoergen leads all winter Olympians with 15 medals that she earned from 2002 to 2018. Her countryman Bjorn Daehlie won 12 between 1992 and 1998. That ranks third of all time. In 2018, the United States won its first Olympic gold medal in cross-country skiing when Jessie Diggins and Kikkan Randall took first in a thrilling team sprint.

Matti Nykanen of Finland swept all three ski jumping medals in 1988. Combined with a gold and silver from 1984, he is the most decorated Olympic ski jumper. Carina Vogt of Germany made history in 2014 by becoming the first Olympic gold medalist in women's ski jumping.

Four men have won three gold medals in Nordic combined. With seven medals across five Olympics, starting in 1994, Austria's Felix Gottwald is the leader. However, Ulrich Wehling of East Germany famously won consecutive gold medals in 1972, 1976, and 1980, when there was only one Nordic combined event at each Olympics.

ABOUT THE COMPETITION

Similar to luge, skeleton racers guide sleds down banked, ice-covered tracks, except they slide headfirst while lying on their chests. The sleds are called skeletons. They can reach 80 miles per hour (129 kmh).

In 2018, South Korea's Yun Sung-Bin earned his country's first gold medal in skeleton.

Skeleton athletes have to get used to their heads being just inches away from the icy track while traveling at high speeds.

ORIGIN

The first skeleton races were held in the late 1800s in St. Moritz, Switzerland. They took place on the famous Cresta Run that travels 1,213 meters (3,980 feet) to the town of Celerina.

THROUGHOUT THE YEARS

For many years, the Cresta Run was the world's only skeleton course. So when the Winter Games were held in St. Moritz in 1928 and 1948, men's skeleton races were included. It wasn't until 2002, when artificial tracks were the norm, that men's and women's skeleton was permanently added to the Olympic program.

ICONS

Great Britain's Lizzy Yarnold became the first skeleton racer to successfully defend an Olympic title when she won back-to-back gold medals in 2014 and 2018. In 2006, Canada's Duff Gibson won the men's gold medal at age 39. That made him the oldest individual gold medalist in Winter Games history.

SKI CROSS AND SNOWBOARDCROSS

A ski cross or snowboardcross race involves a lot of strategy in addition to pure speed.

ABOUT THE COMPETITION

In ski cross and snowboardcross, skiers and snowboarders race against each other rather than against the clock. In both, a pack of athletes starts together at the top of a course. On the way down, they navigate banked turns, jumps, and other elements. The best racers aren't just fast, they're also smart. They use strategy to position themselves against the other competitors.

ORIGIN

Snowboardcross formally began in 1991. The idea for the sport, which is sometimes called boardercross, was loosely based on motocross. In motocross, motorbike riders compete in races with turns and jumps. An equivalent sport for skiing developed in the years that followed.

THROUGHOUT THE YEARS

Men's and women's snowboardcross was added to the Olympics in 2006. The sport was a huge hit. By the end of the year, the IOC voted to add ski cross to the 2010 Olympics.

ICONS

Team USA's Seth Wescott won the first two men's snowboardcross Olympic gold medals. France's Pierre Vaultier won the next two. Canadians have reigned supreme in ski cross, with Ashleigh McIvor, Marielle Thompson, and Kelsey Serwa taking the first three Olympic gold medals on the women's side.

American Seth Wescott, *left*, won his second consecutive Olympic gold medal in snowboardcross in 2010.

SKI AND SNOWBOARD: PARK AND PIPE

American Maddie Bowman works to earn her half-pipe skiing gold medal at the 2014 Olympic Winter Games.

ABOUT THE COMPETITION

Both skiers and snowboarders compete across freestyle events in half-pipe, slopestyle, and big air. Each type of course is different. But all of them have the same goal: to perform the run with the highest-scoring tricks.

A half-pipe is a long, U-shaped course. It looks like the bottom half of a pipe sloping down a hill. Skiers and snowboarders ride up the walls. They perform high-flying tricks as they make their way to the bottom.

A slopestyle course includes several elements, including rails and jumps. The competitors perform tricks on the different features as they make their way to the bottom. Big air takes the huge jumps from slopestyle and isolates them. So a skier or snowboarder rides down a ramp and then goes off a massive jump. The athlete performs the biggest trick he or she can. Riders regularly reach heights of 20 meters (66 feet) off the ground.

Team USA's Joss Christensen performs a trick in the air while competing in slopestyle during 2014.

ORIGIN

Snowboarding developed as an alternative to downhill skiing. Originating in the 1960s, the sport became mainstream by the 1990s. However, for many years snowboarders were shunned or even banned from ski resorts. They had to create their own spaces.

Inspired by the structures used by skateboarders, a group of snowboarders created the first snow half-pipe in 1979 near Lake Tahoe, California. However, the half-pipe was mostly natural terrain. It took many years for half-pipes to become the large, standardized courses we know today. The first half-pipe snowboarding world championships were held in 1983.

Snowboarding was becoming mainstream during the 1990s. At the time, many people figured racing was the sport's competitive future, similar to skiing. However, riders were more interested in half-pipes and terrain parks, such as those used in slopestyle competitions. Many people credit the Winter X Games for helping grow these freestyle events.

Shaun White dominated in the 2010 Olympic men's half-pipe snowboarding competition.

THROUGHOUT THE YEARS

Half-pipe snowboarding was added to the Winter Games in 1998. The event proved to be a hit among fans. Its popularity grew even more after the walls were raised from 3.5 to 6.7 meters (11.5 to 22 feet) at the 2002 Games. The success of this high-flying event opened the door for more freestyle snowboarding and skiing events. In 2014, half-pipe skiing joined snowboarding at the Olympics. That same year, slopestyle made its Olympic debut for both sports. Big air snowboarding was added in 2018. Four years after that, big air skiing was set to join as well.

ICONS

Shaun White set the standard for Olympic half-pipe snowboarding. He won the 2006 gold medal at age 19. Then, in 2010, the Californian threw down such a big first run that his second run was merely a victory lap. Nonetheless, White closed it out with his signature Double McTwist 1260. After falling just short of the 2014 podium, White was back for a third gold medal in 2018. Fellow American Chloe Kim joined him in winning gold that year after an aerial showcase of her own in the women's competition. One of her role models was Kelly Clark, the 2002 gold medalist who also won two bronze medals in the event.

The United States has dominated the freestyle skiing and snowboarding events at the Olympics. Jamie Anderson won slopestyle snowboarding gold in

In 2018, Team USA's Chloe Kim executes a trick in half-pipe snowboarding on her way to a gold medal.

2014 and 2018, plus big air silver in 2018. David Wise won half-pipe skiing gold both years as well. In 2002, Ross Powers, Danny Kass, and JJ Thomas each took home a medal in the men's half-pipe snowboarding event. Twelve years later, slopestyle skiers Joss Christensen, Gus Kenworthy, and Nick Goepper matched that feat.

SNOWBOARD RACING

The Czech Republic's Ester Ledecká races down the course during the 2018 Olympics.

ABOUT THE COMPETITION

Some alpine skiing events have been adapted for snowboarding. The only snowboard racing event in the Olympics is parallel giant slalom. In this competition, riders compete side by side on identical giant slalom courses. Whoever reaches the finish line first wins.

ORIGIN

Snowboarding developed in the United States beginning in the 1960s. For many years, the ski community tried to keep snowboarders off the ski slopes, and snowboarding gained a reputation as an alternative sport. Although freestyle competitions would later become more popular, the first snowboard competition was a race that took place in 1981.

THROUGHOUT THE YEARS

In 1998, snowboarding debuted at the Olympics with a giant slalom event in addition to half-pipe. Four years later, giant slalom was replaced by parallel giant slalom. A parallel slalom event was also included in the 2014 Winter Games.

ICONS

Philipp Schoch of Switzerland is the most successful men's snowboard racer. He won parallel giant slalom gold in 2002 and 2006. In the latter year, he beat his brother Simon Schoch in the final. The Czech Republic's Ester Ledecká made history in 2018 when she won gold in parallel giant slalom snowboarding and super-G skiing. Previous to that, no woman had won gold medals in different sports at the same Olympics.

Switzerland's Philipp Schoch, *right*, races his brother in the men's parallel giant slalom event during the 2006 Winter Games.

SPEED SKATING

ABOUT THE COMPETITION

In speed skating, athletes wearing skates race around a flat, oval track made of ice. Traditional speed skating, also called long track, uses a 400-meter (1,312 foot) track. Most of the races are time trials. Short track speed skating takes place on a 111-meter (364 foot) oval. All the events have packs of skaters who start and race together in unpredictable, fast-paced contests.

Short track races are known for their pack-style racing and exciting finishes.

Team USA's Dan Jansen skates in the 1,000-meter long track race at the 1994 Games in Lillehammer, Norway.

ORIGIN

People in the Netherlands were the first to use ice skates. They skated from town to town on frozen canals as early as the 1200s. Racing took place in the centuries that followed. However, speed skating didn't develop into an organized sport until the 1800s. Short track started in the early 1900s as an alternative for those who didn't have access to a full-size oval. However, it didn't really take hold until the 1970s.

THROUGHOUT THE YEARS

Men's long track has been part of every Winter Games. Women's events were added in 1960. Breaking away from time trials, long track added a mass start event in 2018. The Winter Games in 1992 were the first to include short track speed skating.

ICONS

The Netherlands has proven to be the power in long track speed skating. It's won nearly twice as many medals as the next-best country. Ireen Wüst's 11 Olympic medals are more than any other Dutch athlete. In 2018, she won her fifth gold medal. Sven Kramer of the Netherlands won his ninth medal, and fourth gold, that year as well.

Several notable Americans have also thrived in speed skating. In 1980, Eric Heiden entered five races ranging from 500 to 10,000 meters and won all five. Along the way, he set Olympic or world records at every distance. No other winter Olympian has won five medals in a single Olympics. Bonnie Blair won five gold medals plus a bronze over four Olympics. In 1994, Blair won the 500-meter race for the third Olympics in a row. Previously no woman had won it twice.

Apolo Anton Ohno was a force in popularizing short track. Fans were drawn to the skater, with his trademark bandana and soul patch, as he raced to a gold and silver medal in 2002. By the time he retired after the 2010 Olympics, he had eight medals. China's Wang Meng leads all women in the sport with six short track medals. She won three of her four golds in 2010.

US short track speed skater Apolo Anton Ohno leads his teammates at the 2010 Olympic Winter Games.

The sports don't stop at the closing ceremony of the Olympics. A few weeks after the Olympics end, the Paralympic Games begin. *Para* means "alongside," and the Paralympics are modeled after the Olympics. They have Summer and Winter Games, with each featuring multiple sports. Like the Olympics, the Paralympics have an opening and closing ceremony, and athletes live in a village together. What sets them apart is that the Paralympics are for athletes with disabilities.

Athletes from Japan light the cauldron to start the 2020 Paralympic Games in Tokyo.

Jessica Long dives in to start the 100-meter breaststroke in the 2016 Paralympic Games.

JESSICA LONG

Jessica Long was born without many bones in her feet and lower legs. After 13 months of living in a Russian orphanage, she was adopted by an American family and moved to Maryland. While there, she had her legs amputated below the knees. She also learned to swim. By the time she was 12, Long qualified for her first Paralympics as a swimmer. She won three gold medals in 2004. She continued racking up medals. After competing in her fifth Paralympic Games in 2020, Long had increased her medal count to 29. That made her the second most decorated US Paralympian.

HISTORY

After World War II, many wounded soldiers were adapting to their new lives. In 1948, the first postwar Olympic Games were held in London. The same day the London Games started, 16 veterans in the spinal injuries unit at nearby Stoke-Mandeville Hospital took part in an archery competition. Called the Stoke-Mandeville Games, this event is considered the beginning of the Paralympic movement.

The Stoke-Mandeville Games expanded in the years that followed. In 1960, the first Paralympic Games were held in Rome, Italy. Approximately 400 athletes from 23 countries took part. They competed in sports such as archery, basketball, and swimming. They came together in venues that had been used for the Rome Olympics earlier that year.

The Paralympic Games have been held every four years since then. In 1976, the first Paralympic Winter Games took place. After the first two editions, the Paralympics were held in different cities than the Olympics. However, since the 1988 Summer Games and 1992 Winter Games, the Paralympics have shared the same host city as the preceding Olympics. For the postponed 2020 Paralympic Games in Tokyo, more than 4,000 athletes competed across 540 medal events.

Kathleen Comley from Great Britain eyes her target during the 1960 Paralympic Games.

CLASSIFICATIONS

The Paralympics include events for athletes with different types of impairments. The groupings, among others, include amputee, visual impairment, cerebral palsy, spinal cord injuries, and intellectual disabilities. In addition, there's another group called "les autres." This category is for athletes who don't fit into one of the previous groupings.

Because the severity of impairments can differ, some sports further classify athletes based on their level of impairment. For example, in track and field an athlete who uses a wheelchair races against others also in wheelchairs.

Anton Prokhorov, *center*, of the Russian Paralympic Committee, earned gold in the 100-meter T63 race at the 2020 Paralympics.

Rico Roman, *right*, slips past a South Korean player during the 2018 sled hockey tournament. Team USA went on to win gold.

PARALYMPIC SPORTS

Many Paralympic sports are familiar to Olympics fans. Both Summer Games include sports such as archery, cycling, equestrian, rowing, swimming, and track and field. Some Paralympic sports have major adaptations, such as wheelchair basketball and sitting volleyball. Another adapted sport, wheelchair rugby, is famous for its aggressive gameplay.

RICO ROMAN

In 2007, Rico Roman lost his left leg above the knee while serving with the US Army in Iraq. As part of his recovery, he had an opportunity to try sled hockey. Though he didn't have any experience in the sport, Roman proved to be a natural. In 2014, he helped Team USA win the Paralympic gold medal. Four years later, the team won again. In 2018, nearly a quarter of all US Paralympians were military veterans.

Some sports are unique to the Paralympics. Boccia focuses on athletes' accuracy and muscle control. In this sport, athletes in wheelchairs kick, throw, or use a ramp to get leather balls as close as they can to a white ball sitting on a field.

Goalball is another unique Paralympic sport. This sport started after World War II. It was used as a form of rehabilitation to keep blind soldiers active. Today, it's one of the most well-known team sports for people who have visual impairments. In this game, two teams of three players each face off on a court. They score goals by rolling a ball with bells inside into a net. Goalball has been in the Paralympics since 1976.

Worawut Saengampa of Thailand won gold in the mixed team event for boccia in 2016.

Russia's Marta Zaynullina competes in the cross-country skiing mixed relay in 2018.

Winter sports at the Paralympics include alpine skiing, biathlon, cross-country skiing, sled hockey, snowboarding, and wheelchair curling. These sports are all similar to the ones in the Olympics, but they've been adjusted so people with disabilities can compete. For instance, in alpine skiing, an athlete with a leg impairment will ski downhill with only one ski. That athlete will compete against others with a similar impairment.

A GROWING EVENT

The Paralympics have long been treated as secondary to the Olympics. In 2012, organizers for the London Games decided the two events were more similar than different. They promoted the Paralympics as a major international event featuring elite athletes—just like the Olympics. Instead of focusing on the athletes' disabilities, they highlighted their abilities.

The people of the United Kingdom responded. The London Paralympics sold a record 2.7 million tickets. Millions more watched on TV as a major British broadcaster invested heavily in live coverage. The London Games were seen as a breakthrough for the Paralympics. In the years that followed, more countries and sponsors stepped up their investments in the Paralympics.

Just like the Olympics, the Paralympic Games bring together athletes from all around the world in a celebration of sports.

The IOC often updates which sports are featured in the Games. Here are some early Olympic sports that didn't make it to today's Games.

ROPE CLIMBING

(1896, 1904, 1924, 1932)

Considered a gymnastics event, rope climbing featured athletes trying to climb to the top of a hanging rope as quickly as possible.

Greece's Nikolaos Andriakopoulos competes in the 1896 rope climbing event.

TUG-OF-WAR (1900–1920)

Tug-of-war was an Olympic sport for five editions of the Games. Great Britain proved to be the best at the sport in which teams pulled on a rope, aiming to get the opposing team to budge.

PLUNGE FOR DISTANCE (1904)

In the plunge for distance event, the athlete would dive into the water and travel as far as he could before having to come up for air. The catch was that the athlete could not kick or otherwise propel himself after entering the water. American Bill Dickey claimed the only Olympic gold medal in the sport.

MOTORBOATING (1908)

For just one Olympics, athletes competed in an event featuring different types of boat races.

MILITARY SKI PATROL (1924)

Military ski patrol resembled modern biathlon, with skiers racing and occasionally shooting.

Great Britain's motorboating team hits some waves during the 1908 competition.

The host city of the Olympics designs the gold, silver, and bronze medals.

1896

Dimitrios Loundras of Greece finished third in the gymnastics men's parallel bars. At age ten years and 216 days, he remains the youngest Olympian.

1920

At age 72, Swedish shooter Oscar Swahn competed in three events, making him the oldest Olympian.

1932

Hungary's Aladár Gerevich won his first Olympic gold medal in team saber fencing. Then he won five more, setting the record for longest gold-medal streak in a single event.

1976

Princess Anne of England competed in the equestrian eventing contest. As the daughter of Queen Elizabeth II, she is the most famous of the 38 Olympians who have come from royalty.

2008

American swimmer Michael Phelps won eight medals at the Beijing Games, a record for one Olympics. Those medals were part of his record 28 career medals—23 of them gold, which is also a record.

2012

American Kerri Walsh Jennings won her third Olympic beach volleyball gold medal while one month pregnant with her third child. She is one of 22 women known to have competed in the Games while pregnant.

2012

Canadian equestrian Ian Millar took part in his record tenth, and final, Olympics. His first Olympics was in 1972.

2016

Marathon runners Leila, Liina, and Lily Luik of Estonia became the first set of triplets to compete at the Olympics. Before them, 200 sets of twins had competed in the Games.

Michael Phelps is the most decorated Olympian.

GLOSSARY

amateur
An athlete who is not allowed to earn payment for competing.

amputate
To surgically remove a limb.

banked
Sloped.

boycott
To refuse to participate as a form of protest.

choreograph
To compose the elements within a routine or performance.

coxswain
In rowing, a team member who keeps the boat going straight and manages the crew. The coxswain does not paddle.

demonstration sport
A sport held at the Olympics but for which medals are not awarded.

discipline
A branch of competition within a sport.

endurance
The ability to maintain physical performance over a long period of time.

grappling
Hand-to-hand combat.

mass start
A type of race in which a pack of athletes starts together and races against each other.

propaganda
The spreading of false or misleading information to improve one's reputation.

rivals
Opponents who have a fierce, ongoing competition between each other.

steeplechase
A track-and-field event in which athletes run 3,000 meters (9,843 feet) while jumping over hurdles, some with pools of water behind them.

time trial
A race in which an athlete competes alone and attempts to record a fast time.

upset
An unexpected result when the underdog beats a favorite.

TO LEARN MORE

FURTHER READINGS

Carothers, Thomas. *Great Moments in Olympic Soccer*. Abdo, 2019.

Rule, Heather. *Women in the Olympics*. Abdo, 2018.

The Story of the Olympic Games. Welbeck, 2021.

ONLINE RESOURCES

To learn more about the Olympics, please visit **abdobooklinks.com** or scan this QR code. These links are routinely monitored and updated to provide the most current information available.

INDEX

PHOTO CREDITS

Cover Photos: Mark J. Terrill/AP Images, front (Michael Phelps); Gerry Broome/AP Images, front (Shaun White); Martin Meissner/AP Images, front (Usain Bolt); NewsBase/AP Images, front (Kristi Yamaguchi); Vincent Thian/AP Images, front (Ibtihaj Muhammad); Grigory Sysoev/Sputnik/AP Images, front (Simone Biles); Polina Kobycheva/Alamy, front (Olympic rings); Nikku/Xinhua/Alamy, front (Kōhei Uchimura); Michael Cooper/Getty Images Sport/Getty Images, back (Muhammad Ali); Central Press/Hulton Archive/Getty Images, back (Jesse Owens)

Interior Photos: Francois Nel/Getty Images Sport/Getty Images, 1, 70–71; Hassan Ammar/AP Images, 2–3, 40–41; Sergio Yoneda/Shutterstock Images, 4; Shutterstock Images, 5, 28–29, 33, 65, 106–107, 180, 182–183, 186; Anastasiia Guseva/iStockphoto, 6; AP Images, 7, 8, 9, 48, 57, 88, 90–91, 132–133, 134, 142–143, 145, 174–175, 184, 185; iStockphoto, 10; Martin Meissner/AP Images, 11, 74–75; Rebecca Blackwell/AP Images, 12–13; Red Line Editorial, 14–15, 114–115; Joao Luiz Lima/Shutterstock Images, 16–17; Tony Marshall-EMPICS/PA Images/Getty Images, 17; Anadolu Agency/Getty Images, 18; A. Ricardo/Shutterstock Images, 19, 32, 38, 39, 55, 63, 77, 84; Victor R. Caivano/AP Images, 20–21; Dusan Vranic/AP Images, 22–23; Themba Hadebe/AP Images, 24; Kristy Wigglesworth/AP Images, 24–25, 27; Petr Toman/Shutterstock Images, 26, 28, 44, 54, 58, 59, 67, 104; Marijan Murat/picture-alliance/dpa/AP Images, 30–31; Pascal Rondeau/Allsport/Getty Images Sport/Getty Images, 35; Dmitry Lovetsky/AP Images, 36, 150–151; NurPhoto/Getty Images, 37; John Locher/AP Images, 42, 43; Matt York/AP Images, 45; Jeff Roberson/AP Images, 46–47, 99; Suzanne Vlamis/AP Images, 49; Margaret Bowles/AP Images, 50–51; Dmitri Lovetsky/AP Images, 52–53, 153; Charles Dharapak/AP Images, 56; Darron Cummings/AP Images, 60–61; Lee Jin-man/AP Images, 61, 164–165; Shuji Kajiyama/AP Images, 62; Bernat Armangue/AP Images, 64; Kyodo/AP Images, 66–67, 72, 78–79, 138; David E. Klutho/Sports Illustrated/Getty Images, 68; ullstein bild Dtl./Getty Images, 69; Martin Mejia/AP Images, 71; Leonard Zhukovsky/Shutterstock Images, 72–73, 85, 109, 122, 123, 126, 127, 148, 156; Sergei Grits/AP Images, 80, 136–137; Crosnier/Sipa/AP Images, 81; Julien Behal/AP Images, 82; Sang Tan/AP Images, 83; Anja Niedringhaus/Robert F. Bukaty/AP Images, 87; Red McLendon/AP Images, 89; Lennox McLendon/AP Images, 92–93; Fabio Imhoff/Shutterstock Images, 94; Gregory Bull/AP Images, 95; Manu Fernandez/AP Images, 96–97; Marcio Jose Sanchez/AP Images, 98; Dave Martin/AP Images, 100–101; Mark Humphrey/AP Images, 102–103; Robert F. Bukaty/AP Images, 105; Celso Pupo/Shutterstock Images, 107; Markus Schreiber/AP Images, 108; Katsumi Kasahara/AP Images, 111; Matt Slocum/AP Images, 112, 146–147; Jean Catuffe/Getty Images Sport/Getty Images, 113, 129; Luca Bruno/AP Images, 116–117; Dieter Endlicher/AP Images, 118; Diether Endlicher/AP Images, 119; Charles Krupa/AP Images, 120–121; Tobias Hase/picture-alliance/dpa/AP Images, 124; Iurii Osadchi/Shutterstock Images, 125; Tony Triolo/Sports Illustrated/Getty Images, 128; Mark Baker/AP Images, 130–131; Lionel Cironneau/AP Images, 135, 167; Alexander Zemlianichenko/AP Images, 139; Chris O'Meara/AP Images, 140–141; Adrian Wyld/The Canadian Press/AP Images, 142; Hans Deryk/AP Images, 144; Frank Hoermann/Sven Simon/picture-alliance/dpa/AP Images, 149, 154–155; Don Emmert/AFP/Getty Images, 152; David Davies/AP Images, 157; Matthias Schrader/AP Images, 158; Jae C. Hong/AP Images, 159, 170–171; Andy Wong/AP Images, 160; Mike Egerton/AP Images, 161; Mark J. Terrill/AP Images, 162–163; Michal Kamaryt/CTK/AP Images, 166; Maddie Meyer/Getty Images Sport/Getty Images, 168–169; Thomas Kienzle/AP Images, 169; Marco Ciccolella/Shutterstock Images, 172; Iliya Pitalev/Sputnik/AP Images, 173; Eugene Hoshiko/AP Images, 176–177; Mark Reis/Zuma Wire/Cal Sport Media/AP Images, 178–179; Grigoriy Sisoev/Sputnik/AP Images, 181; Everett Collection/Shutterstock Images, 187

Previously titled The Olympics Encyclopedia for Kids

First Edition
First Printing, 2021

 THIS BOOK CONTAINS
RECYCLED MATERIALS

Editor: Alyssa Sorenson
Series Designer: Colleen McLaren
Cover Designer: Jake Slavik

ISBN: 978-1-952455-07-0 (paperback)

Library of Congress Control Number: 2021917056

Distributed in paperback by North Star Editions, Inc.
2297 Waters Drive
Mendota Heights, MN 55120
www.northstareditions.com

Printed in the United States of America